KD Hill's Chronicles

THE KD HILL CHRONICLES

The Rise of a Legacy

Richard A. Jones

KD Hill's Chronicles

All Rights Reserved, No part of this publication may be reproduced, distributed room transmitted in any form or by any means, including photocopying, recording, or other electronic or mechanical methods without the prior written permission of the publisher except in the case of brief quotations embodied in critical reviews and certain other non-commercial uses permitted by copyright law.

Copyright ©2024

By Richard A. Jones

KD Hill's Chronicles

TABLE OF CONTENTS

INTRODUCTION
CHAPTER ONE: WHO IS KD HILLS
CHAPTER TWO: OPPOSING THE CHANCES
CHAPTER THREE: THE KD HILL'S REASONING
CHAPTER FOUR: THE WAY TO FAME
CHAPTER FIVE: EXTREMELY IMPORTANT OCCASIONS
CHAPTER SIX: LEADERSHIP AND HERITAGE
CHAPTER SEVEN: BEHIND THE CURTAINS
CHAPTER EIGHT: THE KD HILL'S IMPACT
CHAPTER NINE: THE STREET AHEAD
CHAPTER TEN: THE TRADITION OF KD
CONCLUSION

INTRODUCTION

In this present reality where ability frequently meets resistance, and dreams conflict with cruel real factors, KD Hill's process remains as a demonstration of strength, assurance, and a faithful confidence in self. The KD Hill's Narratives: The Ascent of an Inheritance brings you profound into the existence of one of the most momentous figures to at any point leave behind a legacy. This isn't simply a tale about progress; about the preliminaries and wins characterize significance. From humble starting points to worldwide acknowledgment, KD Hill's way has been everything except standard. Through this story, we will investigate the main thrusts behind his persevering quest for greatness. We will inspect the difficulties that molded him, the minutes that tried his cutoff points, and the leap forwards that pushed him into the spotlight. Yet, something beyond retelling a story of accomplishments, this narrative expects to uncover the heart and psyche of the man behind the legend. This book is for any individual who has at any point confronted snags, questioned their own true capacity, or contemplated whether transcending the odds is conceivable. For the visionaries set out to imagine an alternate future and the practitioners who will battle for it. Through KD Hill's story, we will find that significance isn't just about abilityit's about steadiness, penance, and the fortitude to continue to go when the world anticipates that you should stop. As we venture through his life, from his initial days to his ascent as a worldwide symbol, we will dive into the way of thinking that directed him, the standards he held on, and the rugged soul that conveyed him to the zenith of his vocation. This is in excess of a narrative of a man; it's a diagram for anybody endeavoring to leave their own imprint on the planet. In these pages, you will track down motivation, examples, and a strong update that heritages are not fabricated for the time being, they are produced through a long period of persevering exertion and unflinching conviction. Welcome to the narrative of KD Hill's, a genuine encapsulation of the expression, "The ascent of a heritage."

KD Hill's Chronicles

CHAPTER ONE: WHO IS KD HILLS

KD Hill's is a former school football player who played for the College of Mississippi (Ole Miss) and earned respect as a cautious champion. His athletic vocation, in any case, was decisively different after a life changing fender bender in which he experienced serious wounds, at last prompting the removal of his leg. Regardless of the colossal difficulties presented by this mishap, Hill tracked down another reason in life through persuasive talking. Today, KD Hill's utilizes his encounters to rouse others, sharing his account of confidence, tirelessness, and beating difficulty. He talks at schools, temples, and different associations, empowering others to confide in God's direction and to consider life's difficulties to be open doors for development. His discourses resound profoundly with his crowds, as he underlines the significance of finding one's motivation and living with beauty notwithstanding difficulty.

The Early Years
The seed of significance is frequently planted in the most unpretentious of spots. For KD Hill, his story started not in the charm and excitement of a significant city or under the spotlight of distinction, yet in a little, calm town where dreams appeared to be essentially as far off as the stars. It was here, in the unassuming environmental elements of his initial life, that the establishment for a wonderful excursion was laid.

The Modest Starting points
Naturally introduced to unobtrusive conditions, KD Hill's initial years were not even close to charming. His family, however not well off regarding material belongings, was wealthy in values, love, regard, difficult work, and assurance. Raised by guardians who comprehended the significance of steadiness, KD was shown from the get-go that achievement wasn't given to anybody; it was procured, slowly and deliberately. His dad, a technician with a hard working attitude that exceeded all rational limitations, and his mom, a teacher who adjusted the requests of her profession with the sustaining of her family, encapsulated the quintessence of flexibility. KD experienced childhood in an affectionate neighborhood where everybody

knew one another, and the feeling of the local area was solid. The hints of youngsters playing outside, families gathering for picnics, and neighbors helping each other set the vibe for a youth saturated with brotherhood. It was anything but a climate where material abundance was underlined, yet rather the abundance of connections and hard-procured examples. As a youngster, KD's reality was little, restricted to the blocks of his area, the neighborhood school, and the recreation area down the road where he went through innumerable hours playing sports. It was during these early stages that his energy for sports initially started to flourish. He wasn't the greatest or the most grounded, yet he was driven, and that assurance to substantiate himself would turn into a central trait of his life.

Family and Early Impacts
KD's family had a significant effect on the individual he would ultimately turn into. His dad, a man who had worked as long as he can remember with his hands, imparted in him an adoration for difficult work and the comprehension that achievement came through penance and exertion. Notwithstanding the requests of his work, KD's dad was consistently present in his child's life, offering direction, support, and, most importantly, genuinely honorable showing him the significance. Then again, his mom gave the profound establishment to his development. An instructor by calling, she comprehended the force of schooling and the extraordinary effect it could have on one's life. She accentuated the worth of information, tirelessness, and the significance of continuously making progress toward more, never agreeing to unremarkableness. These early illustrations on discipline, strength, and the quest for greatness would shape KD's attitude all through his profession. The Hill's family was likewise known for their nearby connections to the neighborhood local area. They were not just regarded for their hard working attitude and liberality but on the other hand were viewed as mainstays of help during difficult stretches. KD's folks rushed to loan some assistance to anybody out of luck, a quality that KD would convey with him all through his life. This feeling of obligation toward others would later convert into the authority and mentorship jobs he would embrace as he rose to noticeable quality.

KD Hill's Chronicles

The Principal Flash of Aspiration:
However, what was going on was a long way from extreme, their abundance of involvement, insight, and values laid the foundation for KD's desires. From early on, KD was attracted to sports not for the distinction or the acknowledgment, but rather for the test. It was in the serious idea of sports that he originally found where he could propel himself past his cutoff points, demonstrating to others as well as to himself that he was fit for accomplishing significance. From the get go, it wasn't b-ball or football that caught KD's advantage, but instead the nearby leisure activity of baseball. The local children would accumulate at the recreation area after school, shaping stopgap groups, frequently with minimal in excess of an exhausted bat and a worn out ball. There wasn't any need to focus on being awesome; it was tied in with playing with heart and enthusiasm. KD immediately procured a standing as a youngster who never surrendered, who pursued each ball, and who generally played with a fire that put him aside. However, it wasn't simply his athletic capacities that started to sparkle in those early years. KD additionally fostered an intense feeling of administration. While he wasn't the most intense youngster on the block, there was something about his presence that made individuals tune in. Whether it was coordinating his partners in a game or assisting more youthful children with learning the standards, KD had a natural capacity to rouse and direct. Regardless of the delight he found in playing sports, there were additionally numerous snapshots of uncertainty. His area was loaded up with youngsters who fantasized becoming famous, yet the majority of them would miss the mark, derailing life's difficulties or interruptions. KD was very much aware of the cruel real factors that anticipated the individuals who didn't push sufficiently or who weren't sufficiently lucky to get a break. These early battles, these questions, would just fuel his assurance to demonstrate that he could transcend his conditions. It was in these years that KD's attitude started to come to fruition. He wasn't keen on essentially being sufficient, he needed to be awesome. He needed to demonstrate that significance wasn't characterized by where you came from yet by the thing you were ready to forfeit and work for. Chasing after greatness, of breaking liberated from the constraints that the world frequently forced, turned into the main impetus behind all his activities.

The Job of Schooling and Difficult Work

However KD's adoration for sports developed dramatically during his initial years, he never neglected to focus on the significance of schooling. His mom's impact was apparent in his obligation to his examinations. KD knew that without a strong scholastic establishment, his possibilities of making it as an expert competitor would be restricted. The world was not kind to the people who dismissed their schooling, and KD comprehended that sports alone probably won't convey him to where he needed to go. In any event, during the times when his cohorts would kid about his erudite nature or bother him for his emphasis on scholastics, KD stayed undaunted. He adjusted his time among homework and sports, driving himself to succeed in both. His commitment to being balanced assisted him with hanging out in school, where he was known for his athletic capacities as well as for his sharp keenness and devotion to his examinations. As he traveled through his initial school years, KD's normal ability for sports and his scholastic accomplishments started to stand out. His mentors saw the expectation in him, as a competitor, however as somebody with the psychological courage to succeed at the most elevated levels. The mix of his athletic ability and scholarly discipline made him a champion possibility, and obviously his future held something uncommon. In any case, it wasn't simply his scholastic ability that put him aside it was the manner in which he dealt with misfortune. Whether it was managing the tension of school tests, the actual cost of preparing, or the individual battles he confronted growing up, KD confronted each test with a peaceful assurance that turned into a sign of his personality. His capacity to continue to push forward, no matter what the snags, set up for the significance that was to come.

Finding His Actual Potential

As KD entered his teen years, his affection for sports advanced. Never again was he simply a local youngster messing around for entertainment only; he was currently contending at a more significant level, confronting more gifted rivals, and starting to understand that he could make a vocation out of this enthusiasm. His inherent capacities were clear, however what genuinely put him aside from his friends was his unfaltering longing to get to the next level. This drive didn't simply come from needing to succeed, it came from a more profound spot, a position of self-revelation. KD started to comprehend that the way to progress was cleared with difficulties, that the way was rarely straight, and that he would have to outperform every other person to transcend the rest. His initial years, loaded up with battles and wins the same, were just the start of an excursion that would lead him to places he could merely fantasize about around then. The progress from youth to pre-adulthood denoted a defining moment for KD Hill's. It was as of now not just about playing for no particular reason, it was tied in with contending at the most significant level, about building the establishment for a future that, as of now, appeared to be simply reachable. The enthusiasm and responsibility that had driven him to this direction would go on toward being the main impetus in his life, impelling him toward the achievement that lay ahead.

Early Illustrations in Contest
As KD Hills progressed from youth into his high school years, the local park where he went through innumerable hours playing sports turned out to be something other than a sporting space, it turned into a demonstrating ground. Never again was the game played for straightforward pleasure, it was presently about testing one's cutoff points and contending at a more significant level. The serious fire inside him started to consume more splendidly as he confronted adversaries who were similarly as eager for triumph as he was. Yet, what put KD aside wasn't simply his crude ability; it was his savage assurance to win and his conviction that losing was never a choice. Perhaps the earliest example he mastered during these early stages was the significance of mental sturdiness. Whether it was during a local football match-up or on the baseball field, KD immediately understood that ability alone wasn't sufficient. The best players were the people who could figure plainly under tension, who could return quickly from missteps, and who would not allow misfortunes to characterize them. This comprehension of the psychological part of the contest laid the basis for his future achievement. He would proceed to foster a standing for keeping composed under tension, frequently pulling off exceptional accomplishments without giving it much thought. There were as yet many

difficulties to confront. KD's process wasn't without its obstructions. In the same way as other competitors, there were times when his body felt like it couldn't go any further, when wounds took steps to wreck his advancement, and when questions sneaked in. He learned from the beginning that defeating these physical and mental boundaries required something other than difficult work, it required an unflinching faith in his own true capacity.

Mentorship and Good examples
During these years, KD was lucky to have a few key tutors who might assume vital parts in forming his vocation and point of view. These were people who saw potential in him well before he remembered it in himself. One of the main guides KD experienced was his secondary school mentor, a previous school competitor who had seen firsthand the devotion expected to prevail at the most significant levels. Mentor Turner, as KD warmly alluded to him, was a man of not many words, yet his activities said a lot. He was extreme however fair, and he requested nothing not exactly awesome from his players. It was under Mentor Turner's direction that KD started to comprehend what it genuinely intended to be and focused on art. Mentor Turner instructed him that ability was just the start; the genuine work came as training, devotion, and penance. Mentor Turner's impact reached out past the athletic domain. He was the person who originally imparted in KD the significance of authority and obligation. He frequently said, "A genuine pioneer doesn't simply show others how it's done; they rouse people around them to be better, as well." These words stayed with KD all through his profession. Indeed, even in the most extraordinary snapshots of the contest, KD would recall Mentor Turner's recommendation to keep his self-control, remain on track, and lift others up en route. One more critical guide in KD's initial life was his more seasoned cousin, Marcus, who had once been a star competitor by his own doing. Marcus had encountered the highs of accomplishment and the lows of disappointment, and his insight demonstrated significance to KD during crucial points in time in his turn of events. From assisting him with refining his method to offering daily encouragement during difficult stretches, Marcus assumed an essential part in KD's development as both a competitor and an individual. It was through his cousin's direction that KD

took in the significance of lowliness and the benefit of gaining from botches. Marcus frequently reminded him, "Each route is an illustration in mask. Try not to simply win develop."

The Choice to Seek after Sports

When KD arrived at secondary school, it became obvious that he could make a vocation out of sports. His normal physicality, joined with his psychological grit, had started to blow some people's minds. Mentors from adjacent schools started to consider his capacities, and scouts from universities began to show interest. Be that as it may, regardless of this consideration, KD actually ended up at an intersection. He wasn't completely certain if he had any desire to resolve to sports or seek after a more traditional scholarly profession completely. His adoration for learning, supported by his mom, was an area of strength for yet, the possibility of an advanced degree beyond games spoke to him. In his lesser year of secondary school, KD was confronted with a critical choice: Would it be a good idea for him to zero in exclusively on sports and pursue the fantasy about turning into an expert competitor, or would it be advisable for him to keep adjusting his scholastics and think about other vocation ways? The tension was tremendous, as it appeared everybody around him was pushing him toward a future in sports, yet KD realized that the choice was at last his to make. After much examination, he understood that his energy for sports was irrefutable, and his craving to show what he can do on a bigger stage offset any reservations he had. It was as of now that KD settled on the cognizant decision to commit himself completely to his athletic interests. He emptied his entire being into, not set in stone to succeed in manners he had never finished. He realized that this was his opportunity to construct an inheritance for himself's purposes, yet for his family, his local area, and individuals who had upheld him from the beginning.

The Ascent of a Star

As KD's obligation to sports increased, so did his presentation. He succeeded in numerous games, yet ball immediately turned into the focal point of his athletic undertakings. His special blend of size, speed, and deftness made him an awe-inspiring phenomenon on the court. His hard working attitude, sharpened from long periods of devotion in his childhood, put him aside from his companions. While different players could have laid on their normal ability, KD's strive after progress pushed him to prepare more diligently, play more astutely, and consistently look for better approaches to acquire an edge over his opposition. As he entered his senior year of secondary school, KD started to draw consideration from scouts and school selection representatives. His standing as a player with both mental and actual sturdiness developed, and with it came the acknowledgment he had long worked for. Be that as it may, the street was difficult, and there were snapshots of uncertainty en route. It was during these times that KD's initial encounters his family's qualities, the examples from Mentor Turner, and the insight conferred by Marcus kept him grounded. The difficult work and devotion that had described his initial years started to pay off. KD's name showed up in nearby papers, and he began to become well known in the local games scene. In any case, even as he rose to unmistakable quality, he never neglected to focus on the qualities that had molded him. His family's help, his tutors' direction, and his own assurance were the support points that held him up as he explored the strain of secondary school sports.

The Defining moment: A Call to More noteworthy Difficulties
In the spring of his senior year, KD got a deal that would steer his life for eternity: a grant to a lofty school known for its cutthroat games programs. This proposition was an immediate consequence of his steady exhibition and the organization of mentors and scouts who had been following his advancement. Yet, while this grant was a colossal achievement, it wasn't without its difficulties. The strain to prevail at a higher level would be massive, and KD would abandon the solace and commonality of home for another universe of serious contest and new domain. In any case, KD was prepared. The qualities that had been imparted in him all through his life as a youngster, the significance of difficult work, constancy, and trustworthiness would work well for him as he changed from secondary school star to school competitor. His process was simply starting, and the street ahead would be loaded up with the two open doors and hindrances.

KD Hill's Chronicles

However, with each test, KD would develop further, diving more deeply into himself and his true capacity, until one day, the entire world would come to know the name KD Hill.

CHAPTER TWO: OPPOSING THE CHANCES

Throughout everyday life, the genuine proportion of solidarity isn't tracked down in snapshots of win, yet in the manner in which one ascends in the wake of falling. KD Hill's process was never smooth way. It was a progression of snags, questions, and fights both inner and outside that he needed to win. This section narrates his assurance to oppose the chances, transcend misfortune, and cut a way toward significance, regardless of the difficulties that lay ahead.

The Way to School: Venturing out from Home
Subsequent to getting his grant, KD Hill confronted the first of many difficulties, leaving the solace of his old neighborhood and venturing into another world. School life guaranteed new open doors, yet it likewise accompanied a degree of strain and assumptions he had never experienced. The choice to create some distance from his family and natural environmental factors was difficult, however it was essential for his development. The initial not many months were intense. Residing in another city, encompassed by outsiders, KD battled with nostalgia. The security of his family, his area, and the daily practice of his life back home felt far off. In any case, it was likewise a period of significant self-disclosure. He understood that the very characteristics that had characterized him, his hard working attitude, his discipline, and his unwavering assurance were the devices he expected to explore this next part of his life. The underlying battles weren't simply close to home. School sports were on an alternate level, and the opposition was furious. Each player in his group was capable, driven, and hungry for progress. KD immediately wound up confronting rivals who were more grounded, quicker, and more talented than the players he had looked at in secondary school. It was a lowering encounter. His most memorable season at school was a reminder. Without precedent for his life, KD confronted the chance of not being awesome. Be that as it may, this challenge was where his strength would start to sparkle. KD didn't avoid the opposition; all things being equal, he embraced it. He knew that to hang out in this new world, he would need to work harder than any other person. The days were for some time, loaded up with serious

preparation, concentrating on meetings, and group rehearsals. It was debilitating, yet KD didn't say anything negative. He moved toward every day with the outlook that the deterrents in his manner were simply venturing stones to something more prominent.

Fighting Wounds and Misfortunes
As KD sunk into school life, he confronted an obstruction that would test his physical and mental cutoff points, a physical issue. It occurred in his sophomore year, during a critical game that might have impelled him to public consideration. A sharp aggravation in his knee, which had been irritating him for half a month, became excruciating. He had no real option except to leave the game and look for clinical consideration. The conclusion was devastating. The specialist informed him that he had experienced a torn tendon in his knee, a serious physical issue that would require a medical procedure and a long recuperation period. For a worker his entire competitor's life to arrive at this point, the news felt like a devastating blow. Maybe all that he had worked for had been torn away in a moment.
The months that followed were probably the hardest in KD's life. He went through a medical procedure and was put in exercise based recuperation. The recovery cycle was tiresome, and there were days when it felt like he could at no point ever return to the court the same way in the future. His body had deceived him, and interestingly, KD had to confront the truth that his fantasies probably won't work out as expected. Yet, it was at these times of misery that KD's actual person arose. He might have permitted the injury to characterize him, to persuade himself that his time at the center of attention had passed. All things considered, he involved the difficulty as fuel. He pushed through the agony, subscribing to his actual recuperation with a similar power he had once applied to his preparation. His restoration turned into an expansion of his discipline, and each little increase turned into a triumph. KD more deeply studied steadiness and mental guts during his recuperation than he had on the court. It was during this time that he turned out to be very much in the know about the psychological distraction that competitors needed to play. The body could separate, however the psyche, if sufficient, could defeat anything. The injury, in numerous ways,

turned into a surprisingly good development. It constrained him to dial back and reevaluate his way to deal with his profession.

The Battles of Adjusting Scholastics and Sports

While KD was centered around his athletic recuperation, he additionally stood up to the tensions of the scholarly world. The requests of his school courses, combined with his physical recovery, frequently left him feeling overpowered. There were days when the heaviness of his obligations both on and off the field appeared an excessive amount to deal with. He was at this point not the hotshot in a little lake; he was presently contending at a public level, and the scholarly assumptions for his school were similarly as high. There were times when KD questioned his capacity to prevail in the two fields. The restless evenings, the steady shuffling of training plans with task cutoff times, and the strain to perform both on the court and in the homeroom made him question on the off chance that he could really accomplish everything. Be that as it may, each time the uncertainty sneaked in, he helped himself to remember the examples he had gained from his family, his mentors, and his local area back home. He recalled the endless hours spent in his area, rehearsing with his companions, driving himself to improve. He recollected his mom's words about the significance of training, and how each penance she made was for him to get an opportunity at something more noteworthy. He recollected his dad's implicit illustrations in difficult work and honesty. KD understood that achievement was never going to come effectively; it was something that must be battled for, every day of the week.

Conquering Individual Battles and Self-Uncertainty

Past the physical and scholarly difficulties, KD likewise confronted serious unseen conflicts. The strain to succeed both from his mentors and from himself turned out to be practically agonizing now and again. He had consistently valued being serious areas of strength for intellectually, presently, confronted with the truth of his physical issue and the requesting idea of school games, he started to scrutinize his value. There were minutes, particularly late around evening time when he was distant from everyone else with his viewpoints, when the heaviness of his fantasies felt like an unimaginable weight. He contemplated whether he was genuinely fit for arriving at the levels he had imagined for himself. At any point could he have the option to return from this injury? At any point could he arrive at the expert level that appeared to be so inside his grip simply a year prior? These questions tormented him, yet they never totally consumed him.

The defining moment came one day after an especially difficult practice. KD had been propelling himself harder than expected, attempting to get the ball really rolling during his recuperation. He was depleted, genuinely and intellectually depleted, and felt like he had nothing passed on to give. Yet, as he was strolling off the court, Mentor Turner pulled him to the side. He could see the fatigue in KD's eyes, yet he likewise saw something different resolve. "KD," Mentor Turner said, his voice quiet yet firm. "I've seen competitors come and go, yet which isolates the extraordinary ones from the rest is the way they handle minutes like this. You have the ability. We as a whole know that. Yet, you have something different, as well the will to push through when it gets hard. That is the contrast between making it and missing the mark." Those words remained with KD for quite a long time. At that time, he understood that achievement wasn't just about ability, it was about heart, determination, and the capacity to continue going when everything appeared to be self-destructing.

The Way to Reclamation: Recovering His Place
As the months passed, KD proceeded with his restoration and, not entirely set in stone to get back to his max operation. His rebound was slow, and the street was long, yet KD didn't falter. His diligent effort in the exercise center, his steady quest for development, and his assurance to demonstrate to himself as well as other people that he was prepared to do more paid off. By his lesser year, KD had gotten back to the court more grounded than at any other time. His game had advanced. He was quicker, more exact, and had fostered a psychological sturdiness that put him aside from different competitors. His rebound story started to build up some decent forward momentum in the school sports world, and scouts started to pay heed by and by. Be that as it may, what was a higher priority than the consideration was the feeling of individual triumph KD felt each time he ventured onto the court. He had challenged the chances by conquering

injury, however by demonstrating to himself that he had what it took to come back to life and become the competitor he had consistently longed for being. As his last year in school drew closer, KD had established his place as one of the top players in the country. His persistent effort, strength, and steadfast confidence in himself had paid off. However, the street wasn't finished. He actually had another test to confront, the greatest one of all.

The Tradition of Flexibility
As KD remained at the edge of his future, prepared to take on the expert world, he thought back on his excursion and understood that the chances had never been in support of himself. He had battled through wounds, self-uncertainty, and individual battles, and each challenge had just made him more grounded. Something beyond a competitor, KD had turned into an image of strength. His story was one of tirelessness, of challenging assumptions, and of never withdrawing notwithstanding affliction. What KD had realized through every one of the battles was that achievement wasn't just about ability. It was about his decisions consistently the decisions to push through the hard unthinkable. It was about the implicit strength that comes from the inside, the drive to continue to push ahead, in any event, when the way forward was muddled. The genuine trial of character, KD understood, was the manner by which you answered when the world appeared not entirely settled to separate you. As his school profession advanced, KD kept on transcending the numerous obstructions that held him up, declining to allow difficulties to characterize him. Each challenge turned into a venturing stone, each route an illustration learned, and each won a demonstration of the force of versatility. He realized that his process was not even close to finished, however at this point, he had developed into somebody who comprehended what it took to succeed, a competitor who had resisted the chances as well as figured out how to dominate the psychological and profound game that accompanied it. When KD arrived at the finish of his school profession, his standing had developed dramatically. He was at this point not simply a promising competitor; he had turned into an image of assurance and coarseness. His process had propelled the individuals who knew him by and by as well as other people who had followed his ascent from humble starting points to public acknowledgment.

Mentors, scouts, and fans all saw in him something uniquely great a player who had defeated the most difficult of conditions to arrive at the zenith of his game.

The Choice to Go Star: Another Test

As graduation drew nearer, the strain to take his game to a higher level mounted. KD's progress in school had procured him a spot in the expert draft, yet there were as yet many inquiries that waited. Could his school exhibitions mean the expert field? Once more might he at any point adapt to the situation and show what he can do among the best competitors on the planet? The choice to enter the draft was definitely not a simple one. It wasn't just about the chance to play expertly. it was likewise about demonstrating to himself that he was prepared for this next period of his life. For a really long time, KD had pursued the outcome in his game, however presently, the stakes were higher than at any other time. The universe of pro athletics was ferocious, and the opposition was constant. He was going to step into a domain where simply the most elite flourished. In any case, KD had forever been a contender. He had figured out how to flourish, to embrace the test, and to transcend the chances. He realized this was his time. With a blend of energy and anxious expectation, he entered the draft, completely mindful of the difficulties that looked for him, yet in addition positive about the abilities, information, and strength he had worked throughout the long term. The time had come to take all that he had learned and apply it on the most amazing stage.

The Call to Significance

At the point when the day of the draft at last came, KD's nerves were unmistakable. He had experienced so much wounds, mishaps, questions, however presently, the climax of such an extremely long time of difficult work, penance, and assurance was going to unfurl. As his name was called, and the cheers from the group resonated in the air, KD realized that this was something other than an individual triumph. This second was the result of all that he had conquered in his life.

Yet, he likewise comprehended that the genuine work was simply starting. Coming to the expert level was a significant accomplishment, yet supporting accomplishment at that level would be much harder. KD wasn't gullible, he realized that each game, each season would introduce new difficulties. He won't become complacent; he planned to keep pushing forward, similarly as he had done constantly. With that call, KD's expert process started, however his account of opposing the chances was nowhere near finished. He would keep on confronting difficulties both on and off the court that would test him in manners he had never envisioned. However, through everything, one thing stayed clear: KD Hill could fight constantly. He had previously challenged the chances, and he would keep on doing as such however long he played the game he cherished.

Determination: The Core of a Hero
As KD started his expert profession, the way ahead was loaded up with questions. Yet, one thing was sure: he was not a similar individual who had strolled into that school rec center quite a while back. He was more grounded, smarter, and stronger than any time in recent memory. His story was as of now not just about the competitor who conquered a knee injury or the youngster who rose from a humble community to public conspicuousness. It was about the core of a boss, somebody who wouldn't be broken, regardless of what snags held him up. All through his excursion, KD discovered that resisting the chances wasn't just about dominating matches, it was about the demeanor you rejuvenate difficulties. It was tied in with getting up each time you fell, pushing forward when it felt unimaginable, and putting stock in yourself when no other person did. The chances were dependably against him, yet he had figured out how to involve them as fuel. Each difficulty just was not entirely settled. Each uncertainty just reinforced his purpose. As he anticipated the following part in his excursion, KD realized that the best triumphs weren't simply the ones won on the court, they were the ones that came from the inside. The core of a hero wasn't something that could be estimated by insights or honors. It was something more profound, something that had been fashioned through long stretches of penance, battle, and win. Furthermore, with that heart, KD Hill was prepared to confront whatever came straightaway. Regardless of what was in store held, he had previously demonstrated that he could resist the chances.

CHAPTER THREE: THE KD HILL'S REASONING

The KD Hill's reasoning isn't simply a bunch of standards or systems, an approach to everyday life exemplifies strength, confidence, and the steady quest for reason. KD's excursion from school football star to conquering the physical and inner difficulties of a life changing mishap changed his way to deal with life and molded the center convictions he currently shares with crowds. This way of thinking is established in the illustrations gained from difficulty, self-awareness, and a profound confidence in confidence. It fills in as the groundwork of his persuasive addresses and the model he sets for others confronting troublesome conditions.

The Force of Strength: Returning from Affliction
At the core of KD Hill's's way of thinking is strength, a resolute capacity to recuperate from mishaps and push forward even with misfortune. At the point when KD was associated with the staggering mishap that took his leg, he might have effectively surrendered to surrender. The actual injury and the psychological kind of changing in accordance with another truth were overpowering. However, Hill's strength turned into his main thrust. Rather than zeroing in on what he had lost, he diverted his energy toward what he may as yet accomplish. This outlook of versatility wasn't just about making due; it was tied in with flourishing despite difficulties, a topic that runs profound all through his talks.

He's own way of thinking mirrors the rule that difficulties are not the finish of the story yet rather a chance for resurrection. His message to crowds is that disappointment, injury, or hardship is definitely not a long-lasting state, however a transitory obstacle to be survived. An outlook has permitted him to reconstruct his life, to move past the injury of the mishap, and to rouse others to do likewise. This feeling of strength likewise stretches out to the idea of "not stopping" in that frame of mind of difficulty. KD urges individuals to find their inward strength and continue onward, regardless of how troublesome the street ahead may appear. This strength impelled him from being a previous football player with dreams run by injury to turning into an inspirational orator who is welcome to impart his story to thousands.

KD Hill's Chronicles

The real Job: Confiding in a Higher Power
One more mainstay of KD Hill's way of thinking is the job of confidence in exploring life's hardest preliminaries. For Slope, his confidence in God has been the anchor that has kept him grounded, particularly during the most troublesome seasons of his life. Following the mishap, Hill's dependence on God was a solace as well as a directing power. He frequently talks about how his confidence assisted him with adapting to the difficulties of removal and how he accepts that God's presence in his life empowered him to transcend what others could see as unconquerable chances. KD's confidence isn't only hypothetical; it is something he lives out everyday. He urges others to see their own battles from the perspective of confidence, accepting that each hindrance can be changed into a venturing stone toward development and satisfaction. In Hill's view, each test, regardless of how extreme, is a chance for help from above. For KD, God's effortless plays had a functioning impact in his recuperation, his psychological mending, and his capacity to move others. His message of confidence is often joined by private stories about minutes where he felt God's presence, for example, when he was on his deathbed after the mishap, clutching the conviction that he was in good company in his affliction. Through his narrating, Hill conveys the conviction that confidence is an incredible asset that can support you through life's haziest minutes. His way to deal with confidence is comprehensive, encouraging his audience members to open their hearts and trust that they, as well, are important for a more prominent arrangement, whether they completely grasp it.

The Significance of Direction: Living Past Yourself
A focal fundamental of the KD Slope reasoning is living with reason. For Hill's, life isn't just about existing; it is tied in with finding and satisfying a higher calling. This way of thinking has taken on new importance since his mishap. While his football vocation was a critical piece of his life, he immediately understood that his motivation stretched out a long way past the field. His new reason turned out to be clear as he started sharing his story and offering desire to other people. Public talking turned into a way for him to satisfy that reason by helping other people view it as their own. Hill's frequently shares that intention isn't something given to you it is something

that you should search out, through reflection, petition, and a receptiveness to life's lessons. His process embodies that an individual's motivation can develop after some time, and what once appeared to be a professional finishing mishap ended up being the impetus for finding a lot further feeling of satisfaction. For KD, living with reason implies embracing each second and each chance to have an effect. His public talking commitment and his support for confidence and versatility mirror his conviction that object isn't found in terrific accomplishments yet in ordinary activities. Whether addressing a gathering of understudies or taking part in a faith gathering, Hill experiences his motivation by empowering others to track down importance in their lives, no matter what the conditions.

Appreciation and Viewpoint: The Endowment of Life
KD's way of thinking likewise underscores the significance of keeping a viewpoint of appreciation, even despite misfortune. Having lost his leg and got through incalculable difficulties, KD has come to see life through an alternate focal point. He doesn't zero in on what he does not have anymore, yet rather on the valuable open doors that are as yet accessible to him. He talks about how consistently is a gift, a gift that many underestimate until it's past the point of no return. In his talks, Hill's urges his audience members to take on a mentality of appreciation, encouraging them to see the value in the little minutes and not to become involved with the quest for flawlessness or material increase. This viewpoint has been critical to Hill's own recuperating, assisting him with moving from a position of outrage and misfortune to a position of harmony and acknowledgment.

Local area and Backing: The Strength of Connections
One more key part of the KD Hill's reasoning is the possibility that nobody accomplishes significance alone. The significance of local area and backing plays had a critical impact in hill's recuperation. From the snapshot of his mishap, Hill had an organization of individuals including his family, companions, clinical experts, and even outsiders who gave consolation and help en route. KD talks frequently about the fact that encircling oneself with a positive, strong community is so urgent. This thought resounds profoundly in his way of thinking, where he stresses that an individual's

solidarity comes from inside as well as from the connections they work with others. Hill urges people to rest in their local area while confronting difficulties and not to avoid requesting help when required. From this perspective, he sees life as a cooperative exertion, one in which support from others can have a significant effect.

Determination: A Way of thinking of Trust and Strength
The KD Hill reasoning is at last one of trust, strength, and the quest for a daily routine very much experienced. His excursion from a promising competitor to an almost unrealistic man chances and defeated them is a demonstration of the force of strength, confidence, and reason. Hill's message is straightforward yet significant: regardless of the conditions, you can conquer difficulty and carry on with a satisfying life. By confiding in God, tracking down your motivation,

Extending the KD Hill's Reasoning
Going on from the previous conversation, the KD Hill reasoning addresses more parts of life that have molded Hill's own excursion. As we investigate further, we dig further into the topics of initiative, heritage, and administration, parts that expand upon his way of thinking of flexibility, confidence, and reason.

Authority: Showing others how its done
Authority is one of the main features of the KD Hill's reasoning. While many individuals might connect initiative with formal power or title, Hill's sees authority as an obligation to serve and rouse others, no matter what one's conditions or difficulties. His own biography represents this methodology, as he didn't let his physical issues or mishaps characterize his capacity to lead. Following the mishap, KD might have confined himself in his pain or tried not to face his existence. All things considered, he decided to show others how it's done, telling others the best way to explore life's troubles with elegance and assurance. His initiative style is grounded in modesty and the conviction that a pioneer's actual strength lies in elevating others. He centers not around private honors but rather on enabling everyone around him to track down their solidarity and reason. This kind of authority

is established in the standard of worker administration, helping other people accomplish their objectives and understand their true capacity. Hill's message to crowds frequently includes the possibility that authority isn't about position however about impact. He moves individuals to step into positions of authority in their own lives and networks by showing strength notwithstanding difficulty. Hill's authority is additionally obvious by the way he utilizes his foundation to help other people. He frequently urges people to take responsibility for lives, to lead with honesty, and to have a beneficial outcome any place they go.

The Tradition of Determination
One more key component of the KD Hill's reasoning is the idea of inheritance. He frequently talks about how he sees his inheritance, not from the perspective of his accomplishments in football yet through his impact and effect on others' lives. He has discovered that an individual's not entirely set in stone by their material achievement, however by the manner in which they live, the decisions, and the distinction they abandon in the existence of others. After his mishap, Hill started to see life through an alternate point of view. He comprehended that his inheritance could presently not be about football records or on-field exhibitions. All things considered, his heritage became about versatility, about telling others the best way to transcend difficulties, and about being a wellspring of motivation. This change in outlook permitted KD to rethink leaving a significant heritage. Hill's story is an epitome of diligence and strength, two characteristics that he needs to give to other people. He urges individuals to consider their own inheritance not concerning terrific motions but rather by how they impact others with their activities. Leaving a tradition of diligence implies showing individuals that regardless of how extreme life gets, they have the solidarity to continue onward.

Administration and Offering in return
Administration is a vital part of KD's way of thinking. All through his life, Hill has tracked down satisfaction not in that frame of mind, in giving. His confidence in assistance is exhibited through his commitment to talking, where he frequently offers his story and illustrations to help other people.

He is driven by a craving to serve, whether that implies talking at schools, chapels, or army installations, or essentially sharing his message of trust and strength. For Hill, administration is an approach to offering back for the open doors he has had throughout everyday life. He frequently considers the help he got during his recuperation cycle and the effect of the individuals who assisted him with recapturing his solidarity. He sees his capacity to talk and share his story as a chance to pay forward the thoughtfulness and love that others have shown him. This way of thinking of administration is well established in his confidence, as he accepts that genuine satisfaction comes from helping other people. Hill's idea of administration stretches out past his public talking profession. He additionally stresses the significance of little thoughtful gestures, such as paying attention to somebody out of luck, offering an expression of support, or loaning some assistance. These minutes, while apparently unimportant, are amazing assets for making positive change on the planet.

Defeating Self-Uncertainty: The Inward Fight
While KD Hill accentuates the significance of versatility and steadiness, he is likewise open about the battles that accompany defeating self-question. Notwithstanding his prosperity as a persuasive orator and the praise he has gotten for his way of thinking, Hill rushes to recognize the inside fights he has looked in embracing his new situation after the mishap. The way to mental strength was not without its snapshots of weakness, uncertainty, and dread. Hill frequently talks about the psychological fights he faced after the mishap. He considers the deep-seated insecurities and dissatisfaction that emerged as he attempted to conform to existence without a leg. These snapshots of self-question were difficult, however Hill involved them as any open doors to develop. He accepts that defeating self-question is a fundamental piece of the course of individual change and urges others to face their own feelings of trepidation and frailties. By embracing his shortcomings and recognizing his questions, Hill had the option to foster a more significant identity of mindfulness and strength. This course of self-acknowledgement is a foundation of the KD Hill reasoning. Hill exhorts individuals not to avoid their battles or defects yet to deal with them directly, understanding that weakness is many times a pathway to strength.

KD Hill's Chronicles

Building Mental Sturdiness: Strength Past the Body
Mental sturdiness is one more foundation of KD Hill's way of thinking. While actual strength is much of the time celebrated in sports and wellness, Hill contends that psychological strength really permits an individual to endure through life's difficulties. After his mishap, Hill observed that psychological durability was significant to his recuperation. His capacity to keep a positive outlook, to continue to push forward regardless of torment or impediments, assumed a crucial part in his mending cycle. Hill instructs that psychological strength isn't about never feeling agony or uncertainty however about figuring out how to persevere and transcend it. About fostering an outlook won't stop, regardless of the circumstance. For Hill, this psychological durability is developed through confidence, flexibility, and the eagerness to deal with affliction directly. He frequently shares methods for building mental sturdiness, like care, contemplation, and assertions. Hill's recommendation to others is to zero in on the current second and not harp on past disappointments or future feelings of trepidation. Via preparing the brain to remain focused and centered, Hill accepts that anybody can foster the psychological strength important to conquer life's difficulties.

Determination: Carrying on with an Intentional Life
All in all, the KD Hill reasoning is a strong demonstration of the strength of the human soul. It instructs us that flexibility, confidence, and design are the keys to exploring life's challenges and arising more grounded on the opposite side. Hill's process has been one of change a development from a promising competitor to an inspirational orator who moves others to live with reason and strength. Hill's lessons offer a guide for anybody confronting misfortune, showing that regardless of what life tosses at us, we have the influence to transcend. His way of thinking gives an outline to carrying on with a daily existence that is satisfying, significant, and driven by a longing to help other people. Through his model, KD Hill reminds us generally that regardless of how troublesome the street ahead may appear, there is dependably trust, and there is consistently the opportunities for significance.

CHAPTER FOUR: THE WAY TO FAME

The excursion to fame is much of the time depicted as a direct way, a progression of clear achievements that anybody can follow to accomplish distinction, acknowledgment, and achievement. However, for KD Hill, the way was everything except common. His excursion to turning into an easily recognized name was set apart by a blend of crude ability, unwavering assurance, snapshots of uncertainty, and a progression of essential occasions that would eventually lead him to accomplish significance. This part investigates KD Hill's ascent to conspicuousness, following the key minutes that formed his vocation and life, changing him into an image of versatility and tirelessness.

Early Starting points: An Underpinning of Difficult Work
KD Hill's way to fame didn't start on a fantastic stage; it started in the unassuming communities and fields where he previously fostered his adoration for sports. In the same way as other competitors, Hill was attracted to the sport of football quite early in life. In any case, it wasn't simply the actual game that spoke to him; it was the discipline, the design, and the feeling of the local area that accompanied being important for a group. Growing up, Hill grasped the significance of difficult work. Whether it was getting up ahead of schedule for work on, chipping away at his procedure in the offseason, or pushing through the throbbing painfulness that definitely accompanied being a competitor, he never avoided the work expected to succeed. It was this persevering hard working attitude that set the establishment for his later achievement. Hill's initial years were tied in with laying out a mentality that would bring him through each obstruction he experienced making progress toward fame.

Secondary School Magnificence: Ascending Through the Positions
As KD Hills moved into secondary school, his ability ended up being obvious. He stood apart due to his athletic capacity as well as in light of his authority on the field. Mentors, partners, and observers the same observed Hill's abilities and, maybe more critically, his mentality. He wasn't simply the person who could make the huge plays, he was the person who persuaded

others, who worked indefatigably to work on himself and to lift up his group. In secondary school, Hill's became known for his hard working attitude and his obligation to his group. Be that as it may, it wasn't just about football for Hill's. His encounters in secondary school assisted him with developing a more extensive comprehension of authority, penance, and collaboration. The examples he learned on the field would assume a vital part in forming the individual he would turn into. Nonetheless, his ascent to fame was not without its difficulties. Hill confronted difficulty as intense rivalry, wounds, and self-question. Yet, even notwithstanding mishaps, he stayed zeroed in on his objective: to come to a higher level. His capacity to defeat deterrents and keep on taking a stab at significance made him a champion player, at last drawing in the consideration of school selection representatives.

School Football: The Main Huge Break
KD's school years denoted where his athletic profession genuinely started to come to fruition. He was enrolled by the College of Mississippi (Ole Miss), where he would proceed to have a massive effect as a cautious player. School football furnished Hill's with the stage he expected to grandstand his abilities, yet it likewise acquainted him with new difficulties, serious rivalry, better standards, and the tension of satisfying everyone's expectations. At Ole Miss, Hill immediately became well known as an awe-inspiring phenomenon on the edge side of the ball. His champion exhibitions acquired him honors and acknowledgment, however what really put him aside was his capacity to lift the round of everyone around him. Whether it was his hard working attitude by and by or his administration in the storage space, Hill turned out to be something other than a player; he turned into a necessary piece of the group's prosperity. During his time at Ole Miss, Hill's crude ability and enthusiasm for the game made him a fan. Be that as it may, it wasn't just about the game for hill. He comprehended that school football was not just a venturing stone to a possible vocation in the NFL yet additionally a phase that could be useful to him foster the person and mentality important to confront anything that life would toss his direction. It was likewise during this time that Slope started to foster his public persona. He wasn't simply a player on the field, he was a figure who could move others with his words, his activities, and his assurance. He

realized that progress in football wasn't just about making plays; it was about how you stole yourself away from the field, how you communicated with others, and how you took care of misfortune.

The NFL Dreams: Going after the Top

After his effective school vocation, KD fantasies about playing in the NFL were reachable. He had the ability, the experience, and the desire important to come to the most significant level of football. In any case, likewise with most competitors, the progress from school to the stars is nowhere near ensured. The opposition was wild, and he would need to substantiate himself once more. Notwithstanding his earnest attempts, Hill's excursion to the NFL was defaced by mishaps. Wounds, as well as difficulties in the enlisting system, made obstructions that took steps to crash his fantasy. In any case, Hill's versatility, sharpened during long periods of difficult work and constancy, wouldn't permit him to stop. He continued pushing, continued to battle, and kept on preparing with all that he had. Be that as it may, destiny had different plans. Hill's proficient football vocation took an emotional turn when a groundbreaking mishap left him with wounds that would end his fantasy about playing expertly. The way to fame that appeared to be so clear in his school years was unexpectedly hindered. This was not the finish of Hill's story, but it was only the start of another section in his life.

Transforming Misfortune Into Win: Modifying After the Mishap

The mishap that changed KD Hill's life was an overwhelming blow, both genuinely and inwardly. The actual cost was prompt his leg was severed, and his future as a competitor was raised in doubt about. Yet, the profound cost was maybe considerably more testing to survive. For Hill, football had been something beyond a game, it was his personality, his enthusiasm, and his motivation. At the point when that was taken from him, he needed to confront the subject of what his life would resemble pushing ahead. Yet, as I lill himself frequently says, difficulty isn't the stopping point; it is just the start of another excursion. Notwithstanding the apparently unconquerable chances stacked against him, not set in stone to modify. His excursion of recuperation was set apart by both actual restoration and profound close to home mending. He inclined intensely on his confidence, drawing strength from the conviction that there was a higher reason for him past football. As Hill mended, he tracked down another calling persuasive talking. He understood that his account of flexibility, tirelessness, and confidence could act as a motivation to other people who confronted their own difficulties. His message was straightforward yet strong: regardless of how troublesome the excursion might appear, you can constantly track down the solidarity to rise once Hill's way to fame had moved, yet it was no less critical. His new intention was not to engage on the football field however to move and enable others through his words and model. This new section in his life denoted the start of an alternate sort of fame one established in reason, confidence, and the force of the human soul.

The Ascent of Another Inheritance:
In the years that followed his mishap, KD Hill's foundation developed dramatically. He ventured to every part of the nation, talking at schools, houses of worship, and different associations, sharing his account of beating misfortune and his confidence in the influence of confidence. His talks reverberated profoundly with individuals from varying backgrounds, particularly the people who were battling with their very own difficulties. Hill's way to deal with persuasive talking was special. He didn't simply offer maxims or conventional guidance. All things considered, he talked from the heart, sharing the crude, unfiltered subtleties of his own excursion. His weakness made his message much more impressive. He wasn't simply advising others to conquer their obstructions, he was showing them the way that he had done it without anyone's help. Through his talking commitment, he started to construct a heritage that went a long way past football. His message of strength and confidence turned into an encouraging sign for the people who had become lost or who were confronting apparently unrealistic chances. process was at this point not just about private accomplishment; it was tied in with utilizing his foundation to hoist others.

Determination: Another Sort of Fame

KD Hill's Chronicles

KD Hill's way to fame was not a customary one, however in numerous ways, it is significantly more significant than the popularity he would have gathered in the NFL. His process was set apart by beating misfortune, rethinking his motivation, and building an inheritance that keeps on moving others. The examples he has advanced en route the significance of flexibility, confidence, reason, and administration have turned into the groundwork of his new character. However his vocation as an expert competitor was stopped, Slope has tracked down an alternate sort of fame. He might not have accomplished popularity on the football field, yet his message has reached a long way past it, contacting the existence of thousands of individuals. His story is a demonstration of the possibility that genuine fame isn't about honors, records, or public acknowledgment, it is about the effect you have on others, the model you set, and the inheritance you abandon. This excursion from the highs of school football to the lows of individual misfortune and eventually to another type of fame fills in as a strong update that occasionally the best accomplishments come not from what we gain, but rather from how we ascend in the wake of losing everything.

The Shift to Persuasive Speaking:
After his mishap and the resulting end of his football profession, KD Hill's progress from a competitor to an inspirational orator was not prompt yet rather a characteristic development of his own excursion. Understanding that the message he conveyed of strength, steadiness, and self-conviction could rouse others, he left on another section of his vocation: public talking. From the beginning, Hill was reluctant. He didn't see himself as a "speaker" yet, rather as somebody who had encountered life's hardest fights and could share his story to help other people in comparative conditions. His story was crude and unfiltered, he talked about the highs of his profession as well as the lows that almost broke him, including his most obscure days during recuperation. Be that as it may, the second Hill's made that big appearance for his most memorable public discourse, he was met with a staggering reaction. Individuals were attracted to his message as well as to his validness. Obviously Slope had tracked down another calling, one that was comparably strong, while perhaps not all the more thus, than his

experience on the football field. He had the option to interface with crowds such that main somebody who had persevered through evident difficulty could. This was the start of Hill's ascent as a noticeable speaker. Word spread rapidly about the one who had defeated a life changing mishap and presently imparted his insight and point of view to other people. His foundation started to develop as individuals searched him out to convey persuasive addresses at meetings, places of worship, schools, and, surprisingly, corporate occasions. Every discourse was something beyond a discussion, it was a chance for Hill to move, challenge, and elevate others.

Building His Image: From Competitor to Thought Pioneer
While KD Hill's's standing as an inspirational orator was picking up speed, he likewise grasped the significance of building his image. He expected to guarantee that his message came to however many individuals as could reasonably be expected, and for that, he would require a technique that stretched out past talking commitment. Hill started to use web-based entertainment, making content that reverberated with his crowd. His posts frequently a mix of inspirational statements, individual reflections, and experiences into defeating difficulty, turned out to be profoundly famous. He shared recordings of his talks, in the background minutes, and, surprisingly, more private pieces of his recuperation cycle, permitting his supporters to associate with him on a more profound level. By extending his computerized presence, Hill's contacted a worldwide crowd, and his message of strength and confidence started to resonate with individuals from varying backgrounds. As his following developed, Hill's effect extended. He turned out to be something other than a speaker; he turned into an idea chief. His books, online courses, and individual training programs began to arise as normal augmentations of his image. These endeavors not just hardened his situation as a moving figure yet additionally permitted Hill to differentiate his vocation. He could now impact individuals past the limits of his discourses. Whether it was through a book, a virtual entertainment post, or a web-based workshop, KD Hill's was turning into a perceived forerunner in the realm of persuasive talking and self-improvement.

KD Hill's Chronicles

The Job of Confidence in His Excursion to Fame

One of the main variables in KD Hill's ascent to fame has been his immovable confidence. All through his life, and particularly after his mishap, Slope depended on his otherworldly convictions to direct him. His confidence turned into his establishment, giving him the solidarity to continue pushing forward when everything appeared to be lost. Hill frequently talks about how his confidence plays had a focal impact in his recuperation. It was through his faith in a more powerful that he had the option to discover a lasting sense of reconciliation during the most violent seasons of his life. He ascribes a lot of his prosperity and capacity to interface with others to the direction he gets from his confidence. In his discourses, Hill urges individuals to have confidence in an option that could be more significant than themselves and to track down strength in their otherworldly convictions, regardless of their conditions. This profound part is woven all through his own image, from his addresses to his books and then some. Hill's confidence gives him strength as well as provides his message a more profound feeling of motivation. He talks about defeating difficulty, yet about the significance of having an ethical compass, an internal compass, and a profound anchor to direct you through life's hardest minutes.

Breaking Boundaries and Building Associations

As KD Hill's standing kept on developing, he wound up within the sight of high-profile people who shared his obligation to having an effect on the planet. He started to team up with other idea pioneers, including persuasive orator, activists, and business pioneers, who assisted him with enhancing his message and contacting much bigger crowds. These coordinated efforts weren't just about proficient systems administration; they were tied in with making a common vision of positive change. Hill's associated with other people who trusted in the force of flexibility and change, and together, they shaped a local area of people focused on having an effect. Through these connections, Hill's impact extended, and his image turned out to be more inseparable from defeating misfortune as well as with helping other people make enduring change. Besides, Slope's capacity to associate with individuals from various different backgrounds additionally hardened his ascent to fame. Whether addressing a gathering of understudies, a congregation assemblage, or a corporate crowd, He adjusted his message to resound with every particular gathering. His validness and capacity to meet individuals where they were inwardly, intellectually, and profoundly made him a sought-after speaker and consultant.

The Force of Narrating
One of the most convincing parts of KD Hill's ascent to fame is his dominance of narrating. He has the ability to turn his own encounters, regardless of how agonizing or troublesome, into strong examples that others can apply to their own lives. His narration isn't just about relating occasions; it's tied in with removing significance and astuteness from those occasions that can motivate and enable others. In his discourses, Slope frequently relates crucial minutes from his life, from his days on the football field to his recuperation after the mishap. Every story is outlined such that it welcomes the crowd to think about their own lives and perceive how they can apply the illustrations Slope has learned. Whether examining the significance of diligence, the worth of initiative, or the honest strength, Hill's narrating enamors his crowd and has an enduring effect. Narrating is a basic part of Hill's image since it makes a feeling of appeal. His crowd sees themselves in his accounts. They comprehend that Slope's process was difficult and that he, as well, confronted snapshots of uncertainty and dread. Be that as it may, they likewise perceive how he conquered those minutes and developed further as a result of them. Through his narrating, Slope shows his crowd that they, as well, can defeat their battles and arise triumphant.

The Getting through Tradition of KD Hill's:
KD Hill's excursion to fame has been one of noteworthy changes. From a promising football profession cut off by a groundbreaking mishap to turning into an encouraging sign and motivation for many individuals, Hill's way has been everything except ordinary. In any case, this very uniqueness has made him one of the most compelling persuasive orator of his age. Through his flexibility, confidence, and devotion to serving others, he has

made an enduring heritage that rises above the universe of football. His capacity to transcend misfortune, remake his life, and move others has established his place as a cutting edge symbol. Hill's story is a demonstration of the force of the human soul, and his process will keep on rousing ages to come.

KD Hill's Chronicles

CHAPTER FIVE: EXTREMELY IMPORTANT OCCASIONS

In this part, we will investigate the crucial points in time in KD Hill's life that have formed his heritage. These minutes address key defining moments, individual choices, and difficulties that have characterized who Hill's is today. His story is one of win over difficulty, where each pivotal occasion has added to his own and proficient turn of events. From his football profession to the extraordinary mishap that modified his way, and afterward to his ascent as a persuasive orator, KD Hill's life can be perceived as a progression of vital minutes that assisted him with producing his own character and heritage.

The Ascent to Noticeable quality in Football
Prior to turning into a powerful orator and a guide of strength, KD Hill's process started on the football field. His athletic ability and authority capacities were evident right off the bat, both on the secondary school field and during his time in school. Yet, it was his presentation at the College of Alabama, where Hill's turned into a central participant in the group, that undeniable the start of his ascent to notoriety. For Hill, football was not only a game, it was an energy that molded his perspective. He flourished in the group climate, figuring out the worth of discipline, collaboration, and tirelessness. His on-field accomplishments earned consideration, and when he was prepared to enter the NFL draft, Hill was viewed as one of the top possibilities. He was on the cusp of accomplishing the fantasy that numerous competitors seek to playing expertly in the NFL. In any case, the vital turning point preceded he could genuinely satisfy his fantasies in proficient football. It was the appalling mishap that happened in the last option phases of his school vocation, which unexpectedly finished his excursion on the football field.

The Shocking Mishap: A Life changing Second
Hill's life was changed everlastingly when, during a standard instructional course, he experienced an extreme injury that shut down his football profession. The mishap was an actual blow as well as a profound and

mental one too. Hill's had to stand up to the truth that his athletic vocation was finished. For somebody who had devoted such a large amount his life to the game, this was a monstrous misfortune. The vital turning point here was the acknowledgment that Hill's could at no point ever play football in the future, a game that had provided him motivation, heading, and a feeling of having a place. While many would have been crushed and, surprisingly, crushed by such an occasion, Slope's versatility became obvious. This second was a defining moment for him. He might have allowed this misfortune to characterize him, permitting it to keep him from seeking after his future. All things being equal, Slope diverted his agony into assurance. He searched out treatment, both physical and mental, to adapt to the misfortune. His obligation to recuperating was enduring, however what truly stood apart was his capacity to track down new reason despite affliction. This was the principal valid "vital turning point" in Hill's life, a second where the finish of one part constrained him to look forward and rethink his future.

Tracking down Reason Past Football

Whenever Hill had found some peace with his physical issue, he understood that his abilities and interests couldn't be restricted to simply football. He started to ponder how he could utilize his encounters to rouse others. His energy for propelling others developed as he shared his excursion of recuperation and self-awareness. This vital acknowledgment drove Hill to another profession way: persuasive talking. His own battles had given him a novel point of view on defeating impediments, and he immediately perceived that he could utilize this point of view to help other people. He progressed from competitor to well known individual, at first reluctant yet before long understanding that his story could change lives. Hill's message was clear: regardless of the difficulties you face, you can transcend them. His most memorable public addresses were modest. He started talking at neighborhood schools, public venues, and noble cause occasions. It wasn't spectacular, and the groups were little, yet the criticism was strong. Individuals reverberated with Hill's genuineness. They saw him as a previous competitor as well as somebody who had confronted huge difficulties and came out more grounded on the opposite side. His weakness in sharing his process turned into his most noteworthy strength, and his story immediately built up some decent momentum.

The Force of His Most memorable Significant Speaking Commitment:
The extremely important occasion came when Hill was welcome to talk at a public gathering for youthful experts. This was his opportunity to have a bigger effect. It was whenever that Slope first had spoken on a public stage, and the strain was extreme. He was done tending to a little crowd in a nearby school recreation center, he was confronting a horde of thousands of youthful, aggressive people, all enthusiastic for direction and motivation. Hill emptied everything into this discourse. He talked about beating the physical and mental boundaries that had held him down, about finding another reason when all that you assumed you realized about your future is removed. He shared his excursion of self-disclosure, confidence, and the significance of perseverance. Furthermore, the reaction was predominantly sure. That second, that discourse, turned into a pivotal occasion in Hill's vocation as a powerful orator. From that day forward, he would proceed to talk at much bigger occasions, and his foundation would keep on developing. The discourse denoted a change in Hill's profession direction. His standing as a speaker was cemented, and he started to earn a following. The acknowledgment he got from that meeting shot him into the public spotlight. It was at this point not simply a neighborhood local area perceiving his story, it was the more extensive universe of experts, business visionaries, and individuals from varying backgrounds who started to search him out.

Growing His Effect: Books, Web recordings, and Online Substance
One more pivotal turning point in Hill's profession came when he chose to extend his message past live talking commitment. He started composing books, creating on the web courses, and making digital broadcasts, all with an end goal to impart his way of thinking to a much more extensive crowd. The arrival of his most memorable book denoted another section. He took the illustrations he had gained from his excursion and bundled them into a structure that could contact people on an individual level. His book turned into a blockbuster, and the messages inside it reverberated with perusers

who were looking for trust, consolation, and down to earth guidance for beating life's difficulties. The book's prosperity was not just an insistence of Hill's voice as a speaker yet in addition a demonstration of the profundity and effect of his message. Slope likewise started facilitating a famous digital broadcast, where he talked with other idea pioneers, business people, and people who had defeated difficulty in their own lives. The digital broadcast permitted him to additional concrete his job as an idea chief. It gave his devotees admittance to much more instruments and bits of knowledge on the most proficient method to carry on with an existence of direction and strength.

Embracing the Job of a Coach:
As Hill's profession prospered, he started to assume the job of a coach for youngsters. He worked with understudies, youthful experts, and business visionaries who were exploring their own battles. This was a pivotal occasion in his life since it denoted the start of his change from somebody who just shared his story to somebody who effectively formed and directed others toward progress. His mentorship program, what began little, developed rapidly. Hill utilized his own encounters to show youngsters how to fabricate versatility, foster initiative abilities, and figure out the significance of emotional wellness. He stressed that achievement was about accomplishments as well as about how you handle disappointment, misfortunes, and difficulty. Large numbers of Hill's mentees have proceeded to make extraordinary progress in their own fields, and they credit Hill's mentorship for assisting them with understanding their maximum capacity. This period of his profession set his inheritance as a speaker or creator, yet as a genuine pioneer and guide for people in the future.

A Tradition of Motivation and Trust
As Hill's profession kept on advancing, he understood that his work was about something beyond private accomplishment. It was tied in with making a heritage that would move and elevate people in the future. Each vital turning point in his life from his ascent to noticeable quality in football to his recuperation, his progress to talking, and his job as a tutor has been

pointed toward making an enduring effect on the world. Today, Hill's inheritance keeps on developing, as he rouses millions through his books, addresses, web recordings, and mentorship programs. The pivotal occasions in his day to day existence have molded his own process as well as prepared for others to track down trust, reason, and strength notwithstanding difficulty. we investigated the key vital crossroads in KD Hill's life. Every one of these minutes, whether it was the mishap that finished his football vocation, his most memorable significant talking commitment, or his work as a coach assumed a crucial part in forming hill's character and heritage. These snapshots of win, disappointment, and steadiness have constructed the establishment for his fruitful profession as a powerful orator, creator, and coach. Hill's story is one of strength, and his heritage will keep on rousing the people who try to conquer their own difficulties and accomplish significance.

The Job of Local area: Tracking down Strength in Association
After the appalling mishap that finished his football vocation, KD Hill's tracked down strength in his own purpose as well as in individuals around him. In the months that followed the occurrence, Hill understood that he expected to rest on others for help. This was an extremely important occasion on the grounds that, as a previous competitor who had been molded to depend on his own actual strength, conceding the requirement for close to home and local area based help was difficult. Nonetheless, obviously recuperating, both truly and inwardly, was a collaboration. This was when hill found the genuine force of local area. Through the help of family, companions, mentors, and even outsiders who had known about his story, hill had the option to keep up with his psychological and close to home wellbeing. He started to see that mending wasn't just about individual exertion, it was about individuals meeting up and lifting each other up. This feeling of association and common perspective would later turn into a foundation of his way of thinking as a powerful orator. Hill's developing contribution locally prompted another comprehension of administration. He was presently not simply a nonentity in a storage space or on a field; he was currently a local area pioneer, directing others through their own battles. Hill's messages about the significance of keeping up serious areas

of strength for with, remaining associated with others, and building emotionally supportive networks became basic to his addresses and books.

The Introduction of Another Vision: Laying out His Establishment
As Hill's's talking vocation developed, he realize that his own encounters and story couldn't effectively propel people yet could likewise be utilized to roll out substantial improvement. This was another vital turning point: the acknowledgment that he had the power and stage to offer back for a bigger scope. In light of his longing to help other people, hill laid out the KD Hill's Establishment. The establishment's central goal was to help youngsters confronting misfortune, whether that difficulty was connected with wellbeing, monetary status, or individual battles. By making the establishment, hill had the option to set his words in motion. This second denoted the introduction of a more extensive vision: it wasn't sufficient to simply talk about conquering difficulties, Hill needed to effectively set out open doors for the people who were in circumstances like his own. One of the key projects Slope zeroed in on through the establishment was giving grants to youngsters who had encountered life changing conditions. Whether it was because of monetary challenges, sickness, or family injury, he needed to allow others the opportunity to follow their fantasies similarly he had been offered the chance to seek after football. His establishment likewise attempted to advance psychological wellness mindfulness, perceiving that the close to home battles numerous youngsters face are similarly all around as significant as their actual wellbeing. As the establishment developed, Slope had the option to interface with corporate supporters and humanitarians who put stock in his main goal. This was another vital crossroads that not just cemented his job as a persuasive orator yet additionally as a critical figure in friendly effect and generosity. It was as of now not just about private achievement, it was tied in with offering in return and paying forward the potential open doors he had been sufficiently lucky to get.

Confronting and Beating Public Uncertainty:
No ascent to fame is without its difficulties, and for Hill, a vital turning point came when he confronted public uncertainty and incredulity. A few pundits

addressed whether Hill could change from an expert competitor to a fruitful inspirational orator and humanitarian. Was his message real? Did he have the experience and believability to move others? As opposed to contract even with analysis, hill involved it as fuel for his drive. He realize that public discernment was in many cases molded by assumptions, and still up in the air to demonstrate that he was something other than a previous competitor. Hill made a move to talk more, refine his message, and draw in with his crowd on an individual level. As his effect kept on developing, those early pundits started to fall quiet, supplanted by a developing multitude of allies who had seen Slope's change firsthand. This snapshot of public uncertainty constrained hill to go up against his own weaknesses and cemented his faith in the significance of determination. He realize that regardless of the number of individuals that scrutinized his capacity to succeed, he was unable to allow those voices to muffle his central goal. Through his unfaltering obligation to his objective and his certified longing to help other people, hill demonstrated that his process was not characterized by the past yet by the strength he showed in beating difficulty.

The Send off of His Unmistakable Projects: Arriving at Additional Lives
As KD Hill's profession developed, so did his way to deal with rousing others. One more pivotal occasion came when hill started to send off his unmistakable projects, for example, The Strength Diagram and Rugged Mentality. These projects, offered both face to face and on the web, were intended to give people the devices they expected to defeat difficulties and make progress. Hill had forever been somebody who had confidence in the force of significant stages, and these projects were the zenith of long stretches of individual experience and expert knowledge. The projects were based on hill's center ways of thinking flexibility, confidence, initiative, and self-improvement. They incorporated a blend of inspirational discourses, individual stories, and intuitive activities intended to assist people with opening their maximum capacity. Every meeting urged members to search internally, go up against their own hindrances, and move toward change. These projects addressed a higher level of hill's work, permitting him to contact a more extensive crowd. For Slope, this was not just about giving information, it was tied in with making enduring change in the existences of

individuals who followed him. He started to see firsthand the effect his lessons had on people and networks, as numerous members shared accounts of self-awareness and accomplishment.

A Guide and Good example: Forming Future Pioneers
One of hill's most getting through pivotal occasions was the second he embraced his job as a guide. His encounters had formed his capacity to lead, however it was only after he started effectively coaching youngsters that he genuinely saw the force of his impact. He devoted opportunity mentor hoping for pioneers, business visionaries, and change-producers, and this obligation to sustaining the cutting edge would turn into a central quality of his inheritance. Through mentorship, Hill assisted youngsters with exploring the battles they confronted, whether they were managing individual injury, proficient misfortunes, or the difficulties of business venture. His mentorship was not tied in with giving fast arrangements but rather about aiding his mentees foster the apparatuses they expected to track down their own responses and construct flexibility. A considerable lot of Hill's mentees have proceeded to leave their own imprint on the planet, making fruitful organizations, participating in civil rights work, and becoming forerunners by their own doing. This pattern of mentorship and self-awareness is one of hill's most noteworthy commitments to the world, guaranteeing that his inheritance lives on through individuals he has directed.

The Continuous Heritage: An Existence of Direction
Soon after his ascent to unmistakable quality, KD Hill's has not dialed back. He keeps on working energetically, addressing bigger crowds, composing books, and tutoring others. His impact reaches out into numerous aspects of life, from his generous work to his instructive drives and his continuous obligation to psychological well-being support. Hill's persevering through heritage is that of a his man torment into power and utilized his background to help other people open their own true capacity. The vital crossroads of his process were not simply occurrences of defeating difficulty, they were open doors for development, self-revelation, and enduring change. His work has influenced endless people, and his central goal of helping other

people transcend their battles keeps on driving him forward. Through his establishment, his books, his talking commitment, and his mentorship, KD Hill's has demonstrated that versatility isn't simply a characteristic, it's a lifestyle. His story is one of change, one that fills in as a persevering through update that even in the most obscure of times, there is consistently trust and the chance of a more promising time to come. we've dug into the pivotal occasions that molded KD hill's way from a promising football vocation to an encouraging sign for millions. These vital snapshots of difficulty, win, and change play had a significant impact in characterizing hill's personality and heritage. His process is a demonstration of the force of constancy, the strength of local area, and the significance of offering in return. As Hill proceeds to move and lead, his heritage develops, and his impact will without a doubt keep on being felt for a long time into the future.

CHAPTER SIX: LEADERSHIP AND HERITAGE

Administration, in its most genuine structure, rises above the customary limits of impact and authority. It is about more than holding power; it is tied in with motivating others, making enduring change, and making history. On account of KD, their process mirrors a significant comprehension of initiative's subtleties, the way in which it can shape a singular's vocation as well as whole businesses, networks, and people in the future. This digs into the quintessence of KD's initiative and the heritage they are making, an inheritance that proceeds to develop and develop.

The Quintessence of Authority: Reason and Vision
At the core of any extraordinary pioneer lies a profound, unflinching feeling of direction. Initiative is in many cases misconstrued as an element of force or eminence, yet at its center, it is driven by a veritable craving to serve, to direct, and to elevate others. Pioneers who have this feeling of direction act not out of personal circumstance but rather in support of a bigger mission. They comprehend that their choices and activities will reverberate past their own time, and they pursue decisions that mirror this obligation. For KD, authority has forever been tied in with an option that could be more prominent than individual accomplishment. From right off the bat, they comprehended that being in a place of impact implied they could shape the bearing of their industry and, likewise, influence the existences of endless people. Their vision was ground breaking as well as well established in support of others. Whether it was coaching more youthful experts, setting out open doors for underestimated networks, or basically showing others how its done, KD's administration was constantly determined by a hidden mission of strengthening. This feeling of direction directed KD through even the most difficult times in their vocation. When confronted with affliction or apparently unrealistic chances, they depended on their fundamental beliefs and vision to control them through. Their obligation to a higher reason implied they were never influenced by flashing mishaps or outside pressure, as their activities generally mirrored the drawn out objectives they had set for them and individuals they intended to influence.

KD Hill's Chronicles

Visionary Initiative: Seeing Past the Present
To lead successfully, a pioneer should have the capacity to see past the ongoing second to expect future patterns and improvements, and to motivate others to follow that vision. A genuine visionary pioneer doesn't simply respond to the world for all intents and purposes; they shape their general surroundings. Visionary initiative is tied in with making prospects, about thinking for even a second to envision a world that has not yet worked out as expected, and afterward finding definitive ways to make that vision a reality. KD showed this sort of administration from the beginning in their profession. They didn't just pursue directions; they looked to characterize them. Whether it was through their creative ways to deal with business, their strange reasoning notwithstanding difficulties, or their accentuation on ground breaking procedures, KD epitomized the characteristics of a visionary chief. They urged people around them to look past the present and envision a future where their endeavors would make an enduring, significant effect. Visionary pioneers like KD comprehend that their way is frequently offbeat. They won't hesitate to rock the boat, nor are they deflected by the individuals who may not promptly figure out their methodology. KD's administration style was tied in with viewing issues as any open doors for development and advancement. This capacity to see obstructions not as hindrances but rather as venturing stones toward progress was a sign of KD's initiative, and it was one of the key components that put them aside from others in their field.

Initiative As a visual cue: Honesty and Administration
A genuine pioneer doesn't simply provide orders, they show others how it's done. Honesty is the underpinning of such administration. Honesty in authority implies acting in manners that line up with one's qualities, reliably picking common decency over what is simple. An honest pioneer doesn't think twice about their standards, in any event, when confronted with tough choices or enticements. This ethical compass directs their activities and acquires the trust of those they lead. KD's authority was established in respectability. They were not a pioneer who depended entirely on their position; all things considered, they gained the appreciation of everyone around them through their activities. Whether in snapshots of win or

challenge, KD reliably picked the way that lined up with their standards. This undaunted obligation to honesty constructed a profound well of trust with their group, partners, and industry peers. However, uprightness alone isn't sufficient to characterize extraordinary administration. The best chiefs additionally serve others, this is the foundation of worker authority. Worker authority is tied in with zeroing in on the requirements of others, focusing on the prosperity and advancement of colleagues, and it is shared to guarantee that achievement. KD reliably showed worker initiative by coaching others, enabling people around them to develop, and making a culture where coordinated effort and aggregate achievement were focused on over individual increase. Through support of others, KD exemplified an initiative style that motivated steadfastness, cultivated profound associations, and fabricated an inheritance that went past honors and accomplishments. Their readiness to serve everyone around them was necessary to their initiative achievement, as it made a far reaching influence that urged others to embrace comparative qualities in their own proficient lives.

The Tradition of Authority: Working for What's to come
A pioneer's actual heritage isn't just in what they accomplish during their lifetime yet in what they abandon. About making something perseveres, that rises above their time and keeps on affecting people in the future. Heritage is worked over years, once in a while many years, and is the consequence of steady exertion toward a dream, combined with activities that line up with one's qualities. For KD, inheritance has forever been about more than individual achievement; it's tied in with setting out open doors for other people and making history. This is clear in the manner they've coached the up and coming age of pioneers, directed others through testing times, and added to social causes. Their obligation to enable others is the bedrock of their persevering through heritage. At the core of KD's heritage is their devotion to making a superior world. They have worked energetically to guarantee that their impact doesn't stop with their accomplishments yet reaches out into the networks they've affected, the ventures they've assisted with molding, and the lives they've contacted. This attention on maintainable advancement both socially and expertly

guarantees that KD's administration will keep on rousing great into what's to come.

One of the most impressive parts of KD's initiative is their capacity to motivate others to lead. Through their model, KD has engaged endless people to move forward and make a move in their own lives, whether that implies taking on positions of authority, starting social change, or basically acting with additional respectability and vision in their regular activities. KD's heritage, then, isn't simply their very own impressive achievements, however a demonstration of the capacity of one person to light a development, to ignite change that perseveres.

Making a Culture of Initiative

For a pioneer like KD, it's not just about private accomplishment; it's tied in with making a culture of authority. Incredible pioneers comprehend that their prosperity is attached to the progress of those they lead. By cultivating a climate where initiative is empowered at each level, KD has fabricated a culture where others are motivated to assume liability, lead with trustworthiness, and make positive change. This culture of administration stretches out a long way past the bounds of any one association, influencing whole networks, enterprises, and, surprisingly, worldwide drives.

KD's emphasis on making an authority culture is reflected in the manner they've guided and created future pioneers. Through their model and direction, KD has urged people to think fundamentally, act definitively, and lead with reason. By bestowing these qualities, KD has guaranteed that their administration heritage will live on through crafted by others.

The Expanding influence: Initiative That Perseveres

Administration doesn't stop with the individual; it swells outward, affecting others in manners that frequently can't be anticipated. KD's initiative has had this sort of expanding influence. From their initial vocation to their present-day impact, their administration style has motivated people across different businesses, making a tradition of progress that rises above their own time. This far reaching influence is found in the manner KD's mentees and associates have embraced their standards, conveying them forward into their own positions of authority. The upsides of respectability, vision, and administration have gone down through the ages, making another influx of pioneers who are enabled to act with a similar feeling of direction and responsibility. Through these endeavors, KD's initiative has made an enduring inheritance that will keep on rousing people in the future.

The Ageless Idea of Administration

Initiative, at its center, is about impact. It's about the capacity to rouse others to follow a common vision, to act with honesty, and to serve everyone's benefit. KD's way to deal with initiative has reshaped ventures and influenced networks as well as has made an establishment for future pioneers to remain upon. Their heritage, based on a long period of administration, vision, and responsibility, keeps on molding the world in significant ways. As we think about KD's authority, we comprehend that their actual effect lies in what they've achieved, yet in the getting through impact they've abandoned for the people who will follow.

CHAPTER SEVEN: BEHIND THE CURTAINS

Behind each incredible figure is a progression of untold stories, the inconspicuous powers that shape their way, choices, and inevitable inheritance. These stories are frequently stowed away from the public eye, yet they structure the actual texture of the singular's excursion to progress. For KD, the figure that the world knows is just a single part of the entire story. To comprehend the genuine greatness of their impact, it is fundamental for strip back the layers and inspect the complexities that lie in the background.

The Secret Impacts: Early Life and Individual Battles
The way to significance is seldom straight, and for KD, this reality reverberates profoundly. While the world might see the sure, fruitful figure today, the excursion to that point was set apart by a progression of difficulties and individual battles that couple of have seen. Early life was not without its troubles, and KD confronted numerous obstructions that might have stopped others from chasing after their fantasies. A lot of KD's early stages were enjoyed wrestling with a feeling of character and reason. Brought up in a climate where achievement was a consistent however subtle objective, KD learned right off the bat the worth of determination, the significance of flexibility, and the need of confidence. These developmental encounters, however not frequently talked about freely, established the groundwork for the psychological sturdiness and coarseness that would come to characterize KD's authority style. The strain to succeed both from outside assumptions and individual desire was tremendous. While ostensibly formed, KD frequently battled with the heaviness of their own goals. The longing to surpass assumptions and transcend difficulties pushed KD to work enthusiastically, however the cost it took on their own life was critical. Behind the public face, there were snapshots of self-question, feeling of dread toward disappointment, and a consistent inner fight between private satisfaction and outside accomplishment. These minutes, however not well known, were pivotal in framing the individual KD would turn into. It was through exploring these interior and outside

pressures that KD leveled up their initiative skills, figuring out how to offset desire with lowliness and drive with compassion.

The Job of Mentorship and Compelling Figures
In the background of KD's ascent to noticeable quality are an organization of people who assumed significant parts in forming their way of thinking, vocation, and perspective. While KD is known for their autonomous soul, it was through mentorship and the direction of key figures in their day to day existence that a large number of the basic qualities were imparted. Since the beginning, KD had the fortune of experiencing coaches who perceived their true capacity and were ready to offer direction. These tutors were proficient figures as well as private good examples who granted shrewdness on everything from business procedure to individual honesty. They showed KD the significance of persistence, the benefit of building significant connections, and the need to reward the local area. These illustrations, which were many times educated in the tranquil snapshots of reflection as opposed to through traffic signals, have stayed with KD all through their vocation. For KD, mentorship was not a single direction road. As much as they profited from the direction of others, they also assumed the job of guide to the people who emulated their example. This power made a pattern of learning and development that keeps on impacting the more extensive local area they have worked around them. Be that as it may, mentorship isn't generally about direct direction or express counsel. The main impacts frequently come from the individuals who model their way of behaving, those whose talk is cheap. For KD, these figures filled in as both a mirror and a model, showing them what was conceivable and provoking them to live doing the best expectations of authority and honesty.

Individual Forfeits: The Expense of Achievement
Achievement, as KD learned, frequently comes at an individual expense. While their accomplishments might appear to come easily to the rest of the world, the fact of the matter is undeniably more mind boggling. Each step in the right direction in KD's process required penances be it regarding time, connections, or individual prosperity. One of the most troublesome parts of KD's climb was the steady difficult exercise between private life and expert

obligations. The requests of a quickly developing profession implied that time enjoyed with friends and family turned out to be progressively scant. Connections, both heartfelt and familial, were tried as KD's obligation to their work consumed increasingly more of their consideration. This strain among vocation and individual life turned into a focal subject in KD's excursion, compelling them to explore the fragile limits among work and life. However, past the outer penances, there were additional conflicts under the surface that molded KD's way. The strain to keep a public picture while secretly grappling with individual questions and fears was gigantic. On occasion, the heaviness of being at the center of attention felt deplorable, and KD would withdraw from the public eye, looking for comfort in snapshots of calm reflection. These times of self-reflection were fundamental, permitting KD to reorient themselves and return to their central goal with reestablished concentration and lucidity. Notwithstanding these penances, KD stayed focused on their vision, driven by the conviction that the effect they were making on the world merited the individual expense. The inner turmoil between private prosperity and expert desire was a steady propensity all through KD's excursion, yet it likewise energized their strength and assurance to push forward.

The Public Persona versus the Confidential Person
To the world, KD is a pioneer, a nonentity who addresses achievement, development, and power. Their public persona is cautiously organized, an impression of the characteristics that motivate esteem and regard. Be that as it may, in the background lies a confidential person who, however still determined and aggressive, is definitely more complicated and complex than people in general could understand. The strain between the general population and confidential selves is a subject that reverberates profoundly with numerous pioneers. The capacity to keep a predictable public picture while exploring the intricacies of a confidential life can be testing, and for KD, this was no special case. They were frequently compelled to compartmentalize their own battles to fulfill the needs of their expert life. General society frequently saw the cleaned, sure pioneer, while in the background, KD was grappling with the intricacies of keeping up with connections, overseeing pressure, and exploring the tensions of public

examination. One of the critical elements in dealing with this double presence was KD's capacity to separate when essential. While numerous pioneers wind up consumed by their public obligations, KD comprehended the significance of making limits between their public job and individual life. They looked for snapshots of reprieve, minutes when they could re-energize and reflect away from the look of the public eye. These snapshots of isolation were fundamental for keeping up with their psychological and close to home prosperity. However, it was in these confidential minutes that KD additionally tracked down the lucidity and motivation that energized their public accomplishments. As opposed to the outside tensions and assumptions, it was frequently during snapshots of calm reflection that KD had the option to interface most profoundly with their fundamental beliefs, recalibrate their motivation, and pull together on the master plan.

Defeating Difficulty:
Behind each fruitful individual is a progression of hindrances and obstructions that they should beat to accomplish their objectives. For KD, misfortune was not only a progression of outer difficulties; it was likewise a profoundly private fight with self-uncertainty, dread, and disappointment. These difficulties, while seldom examined in broad daylight, assumed a significant part in forming KD into the pioneer they became. Quite possibly the main test KD confronted was the apprehension about disappointment. However they were obviously sure, the truth of driving on such a fabulous scale frequently left KD scrutinizing their choices and capacities. The anxiety toward letting others down, of neglecting to satisfy their own assumptions, was a consistent propensity all through their vocation. It was exclusively through defying these apprehensions head-on, through facing challenges and embracing weakness, that KD had the option to defeat them and push ahead. One more secret battle was the fight with compulsiveness. As a pioneer, KD set elevated requirements for them as well as their group, making progress toward greatness in each undertaking. Notwithstanding, this drive for flawlessness frequently prompted dissatisfaction and burnout, as the mission for perfection turned into a persistent power. Over the long haul, KD figured out how to embrace flaw,

perceiving that genuine advancement comes not from flawlessness but rather from ceaseless improvement and gaining from botches. These battles, while never completely noticeable to the rest of the world, were fundamental to KD's improvement as a pioneer. They formed their capacity to feel for other people, to lead with sympathy, and to develop flexibility despite misfortune. Through these concealed difficulties, KD arose more grounded, more versatile, and more dedicated to their vision than any other time in recent memory.

The Secret Story of Administration
Behind the public exterior of progress lies a lot further, more intricate story. For KD, the excursion to initiative was not just about accomplishments and awards, it was tied in with exploring the interior and outer difficulties that molded their personality. The individual battles, the penances, the snapshots of self-question, and the direction of guides generally assumed a significant part in making the pioneer who remains before the world tod

Going on from the latest relevant point of interest:
The unfurling account of KD's administration, however unpredictably attached to public triumphs, is nowhere near straightforward. Behind each choice made at the center of attention, there were layers of readiness, reflection, and the unseen conflict among reason and strain. These in the background minutes were the fuel that pushed KD forward, guaranteeing that their administration was tied in with arriving at the top as well as about the versatility to stay there, in any event, when the chances were stacked high. As KD developed into a head of impact, there were private and expert minutes that would characterize how they would shape their heritage. This improvement didn't occur in a vacuum, yet rather inside a setting of consistent learning and development. The capacity to adjust to changing conditions and the readiness to go up against the outside as well as the inside powers that influenced their independent direction demonstrated essential to KD's general achievement. Mentorship and joint effort were instrumental all through this excursion, framing the framework whereupon KD's personality and administration reasoning were constructed. From the beginning, KD discovered that initiative was as much about developing

individuals as it was tied in with accomplishing objectives. By getting some margin to sustain associations with individuals around them, KD changed a group dynamic that might have been driven exclusively by contest into one based on common regard and mutual perspective. This shift from progressive reasoning to a more cooperative model would be one of the keys to KD's outcome in the years to come. Notwithstanding, in each snapshot of self-awareness and authority development, the quiet powers of uncertainty and self-reflection assumed a similarly significant part. Indeed, even the most obviously sure people convey questions about their capacity to lead successfully, especially when confronted with hard choices. These snapshots of weakness, however not generally apparent to people in general, were major to KD's turn of events. Rather than the regular story of steadfast strength, KD's process exhibited that genuine initiative comes from triumph as well as from the readiness to recognize weakness and use it as a wellspring of solidarity. As the story of KD's initiative keeps on unfurling, obviously the capacity to offset accomplishment with penance, certainty with lowliness, and vision with compassion will keep on being the principal attributes that mark KD as a head of significant effect. The public awards and expert achievements are positively significant, however it is the untold story of battle, development, and individual advancement in the background that really characterizes the tradition of this wonderful person.

CHAPTER EIGHT: THE KD HILL'S IMPACT

In the realm of persuasive figures, there are some whose effect rises above conventional limits, people whose activities reverberate a long way past their nearby circles, making a permanent imprint on society. The KD Impact is one such peculiarity. It alludes to the extraordinary impact that KD has had, on his nearby local area as well as on the world at large. His presence is felt across different areas, from sports and business to local area commitment and administration advancement. In this section, we investigate how KD's way of thinking, administration, and devotion to self-improvement have developed a remarkable impact that keeps on resounding across ventures and individuals' lives. The expression "impact" itself is a demonstration of the profundity of impact KD oozes, not through simple perceivability or reputation, but rather through his ability to impel change, rouse others, and encourage development. While the KD Impact is complex, it tends to be reduced to a few key subjects: strengthening, mentorship, development, and validness. This section analyzes how these components entwine in his work and the significant ways they have affected people, associations, and developments.

Strengthening: An Impetus for Individual Change
At the center of the KD Impact is strengthening. KD's process has been one of defeating misfortune, stretching through private boundaries, and motivating others to do likewise. Through his talks, composing, and humanitarian work, KD's way of thinking of strengthening reverberates profoundly with people who feel sidelined, whether because of individual battles, fundamental snags, or self-question. His central message is clear: you are equipped for accomplishing significance, regardless of the difficulties you face. KD's ascent from an unsure beginning to progress didn't come without its own arrangement of battles, yet unequivocally these battles have empowered him to talk straightforwardly to the individuals who face comparative impediments. Strengthening isn't simply a trendy expression for KD, it is a core value in his life and authority style. Whether through his corporate drives or his work with minimized networks, KD accepts that everybody has the potential for significance, and his job is to

help other people see and outfit that potential. Through his mentorship programs, KD has shown thousands how to open their inward strength and find the fortitude to follow up on their fantasies. His own story fills in as a guide, a living model that conquering individual difficulty and ascend to success is conceivable. He has frequently spoken about the force of self-conviction and how it is the most vital phase in any excursion. "You need to confide in yourself when no other person does," KD says. This confidence in private organization understanding that achievement starts with the force of decision is fundamental to his strengthening reasoning.

Mentorship: Forming the Heads of Tomorrow
Mentorship is one more essential component of the KD Impact. Since his initial days as a competitor, KD comprehended that achievement is seldom accomplished alone. It needs help, direction, and the sharing of insight from the people who have strolled the way previously. Therefore, KD has made mentorship a foundation of his initiative way of thinking. He trusts in the force of directing others, offering them the devices and information to succeed. Numerous people acknowledge KD for assisting them with professional success as well as with molding their whole perspective. His way to deal with mentorship isn't value-based; it's extraordinary. He works with his mentees to work on their expert lives as well as their own ones. Mentorship, to KD, is tied in with building the entire individual, in addition to the expert. He frequently talks about his own coaches and how their impact molded his reasoning. Quite possibly of the most effective example KD shares is the significance of driving with sympathy. As a tutor, KD underscores the need to figure out the close to home and mental requirements of others. "A pioneer who doesn't comprehend the battles of those they lead won't ever gain quite a bit of favor with them," KD says. "The fact that binds viable initiative makes compassion the magic." This emphasis on sympathetic authority has made a far reaching influence, as a large number of KD's mentees have proceeded to take on comparative practices in their own lives, spreading similar methods of reasoning to other people and developing the local area of pioneers who esteem the capacity to understand anyone on a deeper level and human association.

KD Hill's Chronicles

Development: Reclassifying Limits

KD's impact reaches out past the universe of authority and strengthening. One of the signs of the KD Impact is advancement pushing limits, setting out new open doors, and testing conventional perspectives. KD's capacity to advance should be visible in the different undertakings he has set out on, from tech new businesses to drives pointed toward separating social and monetary hindrances. KD's attitude has forever been one of probability. At the point when he sees a test, he doesn't simply consider it to be a deterrent; he sees a chance to make a novel, new thing. This advancement attitude has driven him to face challenges that numerous others would avoid. His endeavors have crossed ventures and areas, demonstrating that development isn't restricted to one field. Whether fostering an item, constructing an organization, or executing new frameworks inside his current associations, KD has shown that what's to come has a place with the individuals who will embrace change. In his own way of thinking, KD discusses the significance of disappointment as a venturing stone to progress. "On the off chance that you're not coming up short, you're not pushing sufficiently hard," he says. This outlook has impacted the manner in which others approach their own undertakings, empowering a culture of trial and error and strength. Whether through making new tech arrangements or pushing for foundational change in schooling, KD's way to deal with development has turned into a benchmark for some others in the business and initiative world.

Realness: The Groundwork of Impact

Maybe the most persevering part of the KD Impact is validity. KD has clarified that he doesn't have faith in taking cover behind an exterior. He is sincere about his defects, difficulties, and weaknesses, which makes him appealing to those he serves. KD's genuineness is one of the key justifications for why his impact keeps on developing. Individuals are attracted to him since they see somebody who is certified, somebody who strolls the walk, not simply talks the discussion. Realness is an uncommon quality in well known people, however KD has reliably encapsulated it, making it a centerpiece of his administration style. He has frequently examined the significance of remaining consistent with oneself, particularly when outer constraints attempt to mislead one. For KD, this validity isn't just about being genuine with others, yet in addition about remaining grounded in his own qualities and convictions. In his initiative, this legitimacy appears in a profound association with others whether they are partners, mentees, or local area individuals. This validity has made him a confidant forerunner in different circles. His trustworthiness about his own life, battles, and wins has permitted others to consider him to be a figure of power as well as an individual person. This association, based on weakness and transparency, has caused KD's impact profoundly for the people who follow his work.

Growing the Span: Worldwide Effect
While the KD Impact started inside neighborhood networks and associations, its impact has now arrived at worldwide extents. His work in authority, strengthening, mentorship, and advancement has ignited developments all over the planet. From little charities to enormous partnerships, KD's methods of reasoning are currently being executed across various landmasses, making a worldwide gradually expanding influence that indicates that things are not pulling back. As KD's effect extends, he keeps on supporting for frameworks change that focuses on individuals over benefit, local area over contest, and supportability over transient increases. Through his worldwide organizations, he is helping shape a future where initiative is characterized by how well it inspires others and makes positive social change.

The Fate of the KD Impact
Looking forward, the KD Impact gives no indications of lessening. As KD keeps on developing, leading, and motivating, his impact will just develop. His obligation to engage others, sustaining genuine authority, and provoking customary standards will keep on resounding with ages to come. For the people who have followed KD's excursion, the KD Impact isn't just about the achievements of one individual; it's about the aggregate effect that one individual's commitment to administration can have on the world. Through his model, KD has shown that we as a whole have the ability to impact our general surroundings, and that impact is most grounded when it

is established in credibility, compassion, and a guarantee to constant development.

Developing Another Age of Pioneers

The broad effect of KD's impact can likewise be found in his job as a guide to another age of pioneers. His way to deal with initiative improvement is described by a harmony between self-awareness and expert greatness. Large numbers of the individuals who have worked under or close to KD have proceeded to lay out their own fruitful endeavors, conveying with them the examples gained from his way of thinking. His mentorship is customized to meet the particular necessities of every person, guaranteeing that the direction they get is lined up with their own objectives and goals. In any case, what genuinely separates KD is his capacity to motivate others to embrace their initiative potential in a manner that is valid and supportable. This emphasis on long haul development has made a gradually expanding influence. A large number of KD's mentees become forerunners in their particular fields as well as embrace a way of thinking of mentorship themselves. They show preemptive kindness by helping other people rise, which sustains the administration environment KD has developed. As additional people embrace the qualities he upholds, the KD Impact keeps on advancing, stretching out its compass to new areas, districts, and networks.

The Cross-Business Reach: How KD's Impact Molded Different Areas

One of the most striking parts of the KD Impact is its capacity to rise above businesses. In spite of the fact that KD at first became known for his work in a particular field, his effect has spread across different areas. His effect on businesses like innovation, social business ventures, and even amusement addresses his exceptional capacity to associate with different crowds.

Innovation and Advancement

KD's embrace of advancement has prompted critical commitments in the realm of innovation. His capacity to expect future patterns and influence arising advances has situated him as a compelling figure in the tech space.

KD Hill's Chronicles

Whether through joint efforts with tech new companies, his job as a counselor in advancement centers, or his interest in state of the art projects, KD's fingerprints are all around the up and coming age of mechanical arrangements. His emphasis on tackling genuine issues through tech has separated him from numerous others in the field. As opposed to zeroing in exclusively on benefit or business achievement, KD has reliably supported advancements that add to social great, for example, clean energy arrangements and computerized stages pointed toward advancing training.

Social Business venture
KD's obligation to social business has motivated numerous to reevaluate the job of business in the public arena. His endeavors center around making esteem that isn't just monetary yet in addition social. By integrating social obligation into his plans of action, KD has re-imagined being an effective business visionary. Quite possibly his most effective commitment has been in the domain of economical turn of events, where he has pushed for organizations to take on rehearsals that produce benefit as well as advantage society and the climate. Through his administration, KD has demonstrated the way that organizations can flourish without forfeiting their moral obligations.

Diversion and Media
KD's impact in diversion and media is likewise essential. His way to deal with narrating, whether through meetings, narratives, or individual ventures, has reshaped how accounts are made in the public eye. As somebody who comprehends the force of impact, KD has utilized his foundation to intensify significant voices and causes, guaranteeing that his effect reaches a great many individuals. His job as a social innovator in media outlets stretches out past his expert accomplishments; it likewise includes a guarantee to involve media as a device for social change. By cooperating with associations zeroed in on promotion and civil rights, KD has set out open doors for underrepresented networks to share their accounts and encounters on a worldwide stage.

KD Hill's Chronicles

Extending the Impact: The Worldwide Size of the KD Impact

As KD's arrival keeps on extending, his impact presently ranges across landmasses. From North America to Africa, Asia, and Europe, KD's standards of initiative, strengthening, and advancement have been embraced by people and associations around the world. His endeavors to make a worldwide organization of changemakers have prompted the development of various joint efforts pointed toward tending to worldwide difficulties, including neediness, disparity, and environmental change.

Global Effect and Support

KD has turned into a worldwide promoter for fundamental change. Through his associations with global associations, he plays had a critical impact in molding strategies that influence millions. Whether through his work with the Unified Countries, grassroots associations, or global enterprises, KD's voice has intensified endeavors to handle a portion of the world's most major problems. His endeavors to cultivate multifaceted exchange have likewise been huge. By uniting people from various foundations and conviction frameworks, KD has worked with discussions that advance comprehension and solidarity. This worldwide backing has solidified his standing as a forerunner in his field, however a pioneer for the world.

Building a Development: The KD Impact as a Social Peculiarity

As KD's impact developed, so too did the social development encompassing him. The KD Impact is as of now not just about the accomplishments of one individual; it has turned into a social peculiarity that keeps on motivating individuals across the globe. This development, grounded in legitimacy, strengthening, and development, has started a rush of progress that is reshaping society. At the core of this development is the possibility that anybody, no matter what their experience or conditions, can have a significant effect. The KD Impact is an update that the best chiefs are the people who show others how it's done and who lift others as they rise. For KD, achievement isn't tied in with aggregating privately invested money or honors. It is tied in with making an enduring effect.an effect that rises above individual accomplishment and contacts the existences of endless others. This way of thinking has propelled millions to seek after their own variant of achievement, not in light of customary measures, but rather on the capacity to impact the world emphatically.

The Continuous Effect of the KD Impact

As the years go by, KD's heritage keeps on developing. His impact isn't restricted to his accomplishments in his particular field; it extends far into the future, affecting the current age, however ages to come. His administration, methods of reasoning, and obligation to strengthen will keep on rousing future pioneers to emulate his example. What compels the KD Impact so strongly is its immortality. The rules that KD has assembled his vocation on sympathy, legitimacy, strengthening, and development are all inclusive insights that rise above general setting. However long these qualities are maintained, the KD Impact will keep on significantly shaping society into the indefinite future. Eventually, the KD Impact is a demonstration of what one individual can do when they focus on an existence of administration and development. Through his model, KD has shown that genuine initiative isn't tied in with looking for the spotlight, however about making spaces for others to sparkle. His heritage is one of significant effect, in his expert accomplishments, yet in the lives he has contacted and the progressions he has ignited. The KD Impact isn't simply a wave, it is a wave that will keep on molding the course of history for a long time into the future.

CHAPTER NINE: THE STREET AHEAD

Exploring the Future with Reason

As we look toward the future, the street ahead is one of plausibility, development, and change. For the individuals who have followed the excursion of KD, there is a feeling that his impact will just keep on developing, making new pathways for change and progress. The excursion, which started with a progression of individual achievements, has bloomed into an undeniable development that has contacted the existences of innumerable people, associations, and businesses across the globe. However, as critical as the past has been, the street ahead holds significantly more noteworthy commitment. The world is changing at a remarkable rate, driven by progressions in innovation, changes in cultural qualities, and new difficulties that require creative arrangements. The street ahead for KD and those roused by his work will be molded by a continuous obligation to development, cooperation, and groundbreaking authority. This part investigates the ways that lie ahead, the difficulties that should be explored, and the new boondocks of impact that are yet to be investigated.

Expanding on a Tradition of Initiative

One of the focal mainstays of the street ahead is the continuation of initiative that fills in as an impetus for positive change. KD has proactively laid out a wonderful establishment, based on the standards of genuineness, strengthening, and mentorship. However, what's to come isn't about just keeping up with what has been accomplished; about developing administration in manners that are receptive to the necessities of tomorrow. As worldwide difficulties become more complicated, authority should be more versatile and comprehensive. KD's process has validated that authority is tied in with lifting others and establishing conditions where various voices can be heard. The street ahead will be cleared by pioneers who will tune in, learn, and act in manners that benefit the aggregate greatly. KD's obligation to building different, multifaceted networks will keep on being a characterizing element of his heritage, and it will illuminate how future pioneers approach their obligations. Before very long, KD's initiative way of thinking will probably act as a diagram for associations and people trying to make an enduring effect. Whether it's through corporate authority, social business venture, or political promotion, KD's impact will rouse pioneers to think about the primary concern, yet in addition the more extensive social and natural setting in which they work.

Enabling the Up and coming Age of Trend-setters

The street ahead is likewise one that will be formed by the up and coming age of pioneers, scholars, and changemakers. KD has forever been a defender of development in the conventional sense, yet in the manner in which individuals approach the issues of the world. As new advances, social developments, and worldwide difficulties arise, the chance for development develops dramatically. One of the vital parts representing things to come is the means by which innovation will keep on reshaping enterprises. From computerized reasoning and sustainable power to blockchain and biotechnology, the speed of progress is speeding up. The street ahead will require pioneers who can explore these innovative headways while keeping an emphasis on the human side of progress. KD's accentuation on capable development will assume a basic part in directing this change. As organizations and legislatures adjust to the new mechanical scene, KD's voice will be a guiding light in guaranteeing that development serves the benefit of all. Past innovation, there will be a proceeding with center around friendly business as a power for change. In the past couple of years, the ascent of effect driven organizations has reshaped our opinion on progress. The up and coming age of business visionaries will be entrusted with finding answers for the world's most pressing issues, whether that is killing destitution, further developing schooling systems, or tending to environmental change. KD's work in the realm of social business ventures will keep on rousing the people who plan to involve business as a device for social great.

Conquering Arising Difficulties

While the street ahead is brimming with an open door, it won't be without its difficulties. The world faces various issues that require pressing consideration, including environmental change, financial disparity, political polarization, and worldwide wellbeing emergencies. Exploring these difficulties will serious areas of strength for require, inventiveness, and joint effort. In any case, one of the principal attributes of KD's process is his capacity to transform difficulties into amazing open doors. This attitude will be significant as he keeps on directing others in dealing with the complicated issues that lie ahead. For instance, environmental change addresses one of the most major problems representing things to come. The worldwide local area should cooperate to track down supportable arrangements, and coordinated effort will be vital to progress. KD has reliably accentuated the significance of organizations in accomplishing long haul change. Whether it's through corporate partnerships, NGOs, or government drives, the street ahead will require remarkable degrees of participation. KD's way of thinking of spanning partitions and uniting different partners will be fundamental in conquering the difficulties presented by a quickly evolving climate. Financial disparity is one more issue that will keep on molding the street ahead. The hole between the rich and the poor is enlarging, and this uniqueness is felt all the more intensely in agricultural nations and disappointed networks. KD's work with underserved populaces will take on new significance as pioneers track down ways of handling foundational disparity. Whether it's through comprehensive training, position creation, or widespread medical care, the future will request inventive arrangements that address the underlying drivers of disparity.

Molding a Worldwide Development for Good

As the world turns out to be more interconnected, the street ahead will likewise be molded by the ascent of worldwide developments for equity, equity, and manageability. The force of virtual entertainment and computerized stages has previously changed how social developments work, and this pattern will just proceed. KD's work has forever been centered around building networks that are joined by a typical reason. Pushing ahead, he will keep on being a main impetus in encouraging worldwide fortitude among different gatherings who share a dream for a superior future. The ascent of computerized activism and worldwide support organizations will give common residents more power than any time in recent memory to influence change. KD's voice in these worldwide developments will keep on being vital in preparing people and associations to act in manners that make fundamental change. Whether upholding for common freedoms, ecological supportability, or orientation uniformity, KD's impact will keep on powering a worldwide development for positive change.

The Job of Self-awareness in the Street Ahead
One of the most significant parts of KD's inheritance is his obligation to self-awareness. As the world changes, it's fundamental that people keep on advancing, adjust, and fill to address the difficulties representing things to come. KD has forever been a boss of ceaseless personal growth, and this will stay a vital subject in the years to come. Self-improvement isn't just about obtaining new abilities or information, yet in addition about fostering the capacity to understand people on a deeper level and strength expected to explore a perplexing world. KD's own excursion of individual change will keep on moving people to focus on deep rooted learning and self-disclosure. As new difficulties arise, the individuals who have embraced self-awareness will be better prepared to track down arrangements, lead with sympathy, and adjust to evolving conditions.

Determination: A Future Characterized by Reason
The street ahead is one of limitless potential, yet likewise one requires deliberateness and reason. The way that KD has spread out isn't one that drives exclusively to individual achievement or acknowledgment. A way is centered around administration, strengthening, and making enduring change. The future will request pioneers who are focused on these standards, who will develop, team up, and make a strong move despite vulnerability. For KD, the street ahead isn't tied in with laying on past achievements it's tied in with proceeding with the excursion of development, impact, and effect. He will stay a voice for positive change, a coach to future pioneers, and a wellspring of motivation for those looking to have an effect on the planet. As the world faces an undeniably complicated and interconnected future, the examples of the KD Impact will keep on resounding. Through his visionary administration, obligation to self-awareness, and relentless devotion to social great, KD's impact will assist with molding the street ahead, lighting the way for the people who

are prepared to emulate his example and make a superior world for a long time into the future.

The Job of Worldwide Coordinated effort

What was to come, molded by both open door and challenge, will progressively be characterized by worldwide joint effort. The interconnected idea of the present world implies that issues are not generally segregated to one district or area. The street ahead will require a feeling of worldwide collaboration, where shared objectives, whether natural supportability, mechanical headway, or harmony building outweigh public limits. One region where this is particularly significant is in handling environmental change. Nations all over the planet have perceived the dire requirement for bound together activity to battle a dangerous atmospheric deviation and ecological corruption. This requires a multi-partner approach, with legislatures, organizations, and grassroots associations meeting up to make arrangements. The KD Impact, portrayed by a guarantee to comprehensive authority, will assume an essential part in forming future organizations across the globe. KD's tradition of building spans between apparently different gatherings can act as a model for global participation. His attention on understanding alternate points of view and figuring out something worth agreeing on, even amidst conflict, will be fundamental as worldwide foundations cooperate to address the world's most major problems.

The Requirement for Tough Authority

One more key part of the street ahead is the requirement for strong initiative. The difficulties representing things to come are probably going to be both surprising and significant, and the individuals who lead should explore vulnerability with strength and flexibility. Versatility will be a basic quality for pioneers, despite emergency, yet in addition in the continuous course of development and advancement. KD's initiative has forever been established in flexibility, as an individual quality as well as a worth that he has imparted in others. Later on, as ventures face interruptions whether from mechanical progressions, international strains, or cultural movements flexibility will be the foundation of fruitful administration. The capacity to turn, gain from disappointment, and remain grounded in one's qualities will be fundamental for defeating the snags that lie ahead. Besides, the emphasis on psychological wellness and close to home prosperity in authority is progressively significant. Heads of tomorrow should be as aware of their close to home wellbeing as they are of their business techniques. The self-improvement that KD has supported will stretch out into the close to home domain, with an emphasis on compassion, mindfulness, and realness characteristics that will characterize the up and coming age of pioneers.

Cultivating Inventiveness and Advancement
As we push ahead, imagination and development will be the motors that drive progress. The issues of tomorrow are probably going to be diverse and complex, requiring better approaches for thinking. The future won't be molded by the people who stick to obsolete models yet by the individuals who try to break new ground, challenge customary standards, and really ponder additional opportunities. KD's impact in cultivating a culture of imaginative reasoning will keep on moving future pioneers to look for creative answers for worldwide difficulties. His own process has been set apart by a readiness to face challenges, to explore different avenues regarding whimsical thoughts, and to rock the boat. As the world faces the requirement for extremist arrangements whether in energy, medical care, or schooling KD's model will move others to push limits and make change in extraordinary ways. The rising significance of interdisciplinary coordinated effort will likewise assume an essential part in cultivating development. By uniting people with different abilities, information, and encounters, the upcoming pioneers will actually want to handle complex issues from numerous points. The future will see the combination of fields like innovation, science, and artistic expression, all cooperating to take care of issues in manners that were beforehand impossible.

Taking part in Worldwide Citizenship
As we look forward, the idea of worldwide citizenship will turn out to be more significant. In a world that is progressively interconnected, the choices made in one piece of the globe can have expansive ramifications

for different regions of the planet. Future pioneers should think past public interests and think about the worldwide effect of their activities. This thought of worldwide obligation lines up with the qualities KD has advanced all through his profession. He has underscored the significance of taking responsibility for activities and the aggregate effect we have on the world. The street ahead will require another variety of pioneers who are not simply worried about the outcome of their own organizations or nations, however who figure out their job in the more extensive worldwide environment. To completely embrace worldwide citizenship, pioneers should focus on joint effort over contests. This implies cooperating to address worldwide emergencies, yet additionally long haul objectives like destitution mitigation, schooling access, and worldwide wellbeing. KD's progress centered around enabling others and making comprehensive spaces will be significant as people across the world work to construct an all the more and even handed society.

Reconsidering the Fate of Work
The fate of work is a subject that keeps on developing, particularly considering innovative progressions and changing cultural assumptions. The ascent of mechanization, man-made brainpower, and remote work are reshaping the labor force, introducing the two difficulties and amazing open doors. Heads representing things to come should establish conditions where innovation supplements human imagination and ability, as opposed to supplanting it. The street ahead will request a reconsidering of work, where individuals' jobs are constantly developing, and potential open doors for development are open to all. Future pioneers should embrace adaptability, variety, and deep rooted figuring out how to guarantee that the labor force stays versatile to evolving conditions. KD's faith in the force of self-improvement lines up with this vision representing things to come. By advocating long lasting acquiring and abilities improvement, future pioneers will actually want to explore the changing scene of work with certainty. Also, making comprehensive work environments that advance value and balance between serious and fun activities will be fundamental for drawing in and holding top ability in the years to come.

KD Hill's Chronicles

Trustworthy driving
Most importantly, the street ahead will expect pioneers to act with uprightness. In our current reality where trust is progressively hard to find, the pioneers who adapt to the situation will be the people who work with straightforwardness, genuineness, and an unfaltering obligation to moral way of behaving. KD has reliably exhibited the force of driving with honesty. His activities have forever been directed by his qualities, and he has shown that genuine administration isn't tied in with looking for acknowledgment, yet about making the right decision, in any event, when nobody is watching. This emphasis on honesty will be a higher priority than any time in recent memory as the world faces progressively complex moral quandaries in regions like protection, innovation, and civil rights. The pioneers who prevail in the street ahead will be the people who focus on trust-building and responsibility, perceiving that administration isn't just about accomplishing objectives, however about doing as such that regards the poise and privileges of others. The KD Impact will keep on rousing people to lead with their psyches as well as with their souls, pursuing choices that benefit everyone's benefit and maintaining the honest best expectations.

The Street Ahead is Simply Starting
As we look forward, obviously the street isn't simply a continuation of the past, it's another outskirts, loaded with undiscovered possibility. The examples that KD has conferred will keep on molding how future pioneers approach difficulties, amazing open doors, and self-improvement. His impact won't blur with time, however will rather proceed to rouse and direct people across the globe. The street ahead might be long, however one will be cleared by the individuals who lead with reason, who embrace advancement, who esteem trustworthiness, and who grasp the significance of coordinated effort. As KD's process keeps on unfurling, his heritage will motivate another age of pioneers to rise, change, and fabricate a future that is more splendid, more comprehensive, and more reasonable. The street ahead is brimming with commitment, and the people who are prepared to walk it, with KD's lessons as their aide, will shape the future in manners that are yet to be envisioned. The excursion is simply starting, and the KD

KD Hill's Chronicles

Impact will keep on undulating outward, influencing the world one pioneer, one development, and with care.

CHAPTER TEN: THE TRADITION OF KD

As the excursion advances, one thing turns out to be clear: the tradition of KD isn't simply characterized by achievements or awards, but by the significant effect on the people who have encountered them, on the networks they have contacted, and on the frameworks they have reshaped. KD's impact reaches out a long ways past their own accomplishments. It is woven into the texture of the ventures they have changed, individuals they have roused, and the developments they have started. This part investigates the complex idea of this persevering through inheritance, its expansive impacts, and how it will keep on resounding for a long time into the future.

Characterizing the Center of the Inheritance
An inheritance is many times seen from the perspective of substantial achievements: the organizations constructed, the developments presented, or the achievements accomplished. While KD has unquestionably amassed a noteworthy rundown of individual triumphs, their actual heritage lies in the qualities they have conferred to the world and the standards they have lived by. The bedrock of this inheritance is focused on a few key topics: flexibility, development, inclusivity, and reason driven initiative. These standards have molded KD's vocation as well as have filled in as the diagram for the people who have emulated their example. Through a pledge to showing others how it's done, KD has shown that achievement isn't just about private accomplishment, but about making a significant far reaching influence that can change lives, rouse others, and add to the benefit of everyone.

The Expanding influence: Enabling Others
One of the most significant components of KD's heritage is the capacity to engage others. Whether through mentorship, shared astuteness, or basically showing others how it's done, KD's methodology has been one that encourages development in others. This approach isn't just about giving individuals the instruments to succeed; it is about ingraining the certainty to embrace difficulties, to push limits, and to advance persistently.

KD Hill's Chronicles

Mentorship has been a focal part of KD's way of thinking. Whether straightforwardly or by implication, KD has coached incalculable people, sharing experiences, giving direction, and assisting with molding the up and coming age of pioneers. The spotlight has forever been on individual development, guaranteeing that the people who are coached don't just recreate KD's process yet cut out their own ways utilizing the instruments they have been given. In the long haul, this approach has prompted a multiplier impact. The people who were once guided have proceeded to coach others, making a local area of pioneers who share similar qualities and vision. This propagation of information and strengthening guarantees that KD's effect won't blur with time, however , it will keep on resounding long after their immediate impact has finished.

Development and Change
The core of KD's heritage lies in the capacity to advance. In the mechanical or negotiating prudence, yet by they way they moved toward issues, difficulties, and valuable open doors. KD's vocation has been set apart by a refusal to acknowledge the state of affairs and an unflinching obligation to testing the customary way of thinking. This mentality of troublesome development has been a foundation of their heritage. In business, KD has upset ventures through strong, whimsical reasoning. In administration, they have shown that advancement isn't exclusively about making new items or administrations, however about reconsidering the state of affairs done. This incorporates reconsidering corporate designs, reclassifying hierarchical culture, and addressing obsolete practices for more proficient, compelling, and accommodating arrangements. Development, for KD, isn't just about the outcome; it's tied in with cultivating a culture of constant improvement. It's tied in with empowering others to take a gander at issues from new points, to investigate new advances, and to never agree to "sufficient." This outlook has made a permanent imprint on enterprises and areas a long way past KD's own proficient circle. It has propelled incalculable people and associations to think all the more inventively, act with more noteworthy boldness, and embrace the chance of extremist change.

Administration with Reason

KD Hill's Chronicles

The genuine quintessence of authority, as exemplified by KD, is grounded in reason. For KD, administration was never about the title or the acknowledgment. It was consistently about having an effect, whether through friendly change, financial change, or self-awareness. This reason driven initiative has gained KD appreciation inside their field as well as has made them an image of leading with respectability, enthusiasm, and a promise to everyone's benefit. Intention has supported KD through the unavoidable difficulties and misfortunes that all chiefs face. It has kept them grounded in snapshots of achievement and has moved them forward in the midst of difficulty. By remaining consistent with their qualities and keeping a reasonable internal compass, KD has shown that initiative isn't just about having a dream, yet about making an interpretation of that vision into significant activity. This obligation to reason driven initiative affects the associations and networks KD has worked with. By imparting a feeling of direction in their groups, KD has established conditions where people are propelled by monetary motivators or individual addition, however by an aggregate vision that lines up with their fundamental beliefs. This has prompted more significant levels of commitment, more noteworthy work fulfillment, and a persevering through obligation to accomplish long haul objectives.

Social and Social Effect
The tradition of KD reaches out past the expert and business domains into the more extensive social and social scenes. KD has forever been keenly conscious about the force of impact and has utilized it to lift significant causes and to address cultural difficulties. Their promotion for civil rights, value, and local area commitment has been a critical piece of their enduring effect. Through different stages, KD has reliably utilized their voice to support underrepresented gatherings, to address foundational imbalances, and to push for change in regions like schooling, medical services, and monetary open door. By utilizing their leverage for good, KD has turned into a power for positive social change, empowering others to move forward and get a sense of ownership with their networks. One of the most getting through parts of KD's inheritance will be the way of life of inclusivity they have encouraged. By embracing individuals from varying

backgrounds, KD has shown that genuine authority isn't about prohibition or elitism, but about inviting different points of view and building frameworks that benefit everybody. This approach has prompted more comprehensive work environments, more prominent admittance to amazing open doors, and a continuous discourse about the significance of social value.

The Drawn out Effect: Forming Ages
As we plan ahead, the full degree of KD's heritage will keep on unfurling. The standards they have advocated for strength, advancement, reason driven administration, and inclusivity will keep on forming the activities and choices of future pioneers. The gradually expanding influence of KD's impact will be felt in ages to come, as the people who have been moved by their administration keep on expanding on the establishment they have set. The drawn out effect of KD's inheritance isn't just about the progressions they have made yet about the attitude they have developed. A mentality that won't acknowledge limits, that trusts in that frame of mind of change, and that holds the possibility to reshape the world in manners we still can't seem to envision. KD's heritage will likewise be one of enduring motivation. Their story will keep on filling in as a signal for the people who try to have an effect, for the individuals who seek to lead with reason, and for the people who put stock in the chance of progress. The street ahead might be dubious, however the tradition of KD will keep on lighting the way for the individuals who follow.

The Incomplete Excursion:
In numerous ways, the narrative of KD is as yet unfurling. While their heritage is now profoundly dug in on the planet they have changed, obviously their impact will keep on developing, advancing, and moving people in the future. The street ahead is long, however KD's excursion, characterized by flexibility, advancement, and intention, is nowhere near finished. As we ponder KD's heritage, obviously it's anything but a static accomplishment however a no nonsense power, one that will keep on moving, challenge, and push future pioneers to arrive at more prominent levels. Through the tales, activities, and effect KD abandons, their heritage will live on, filling in as both an aide and a motivation for the people who

endeavor to leave behind a legacy. The tradition of KD isn't just about what they have achieved however about what they have propelled others to do. It is a heritage constructed not on private victories alone, but rather on the aggregate development and strengthening of the people who have emulated their example. Furthermore, as the world keeps on changing, so too will KD's inheritance continuously developing, consistently significant, and consistently a directing power for people in the future. As KD's impact keeps on reverberating all through the ventures they've contacted, it's obvious that their heritage won't just persevere however flourish in that frame of mind of the people who follow. While their process has been set apart by endless achievements, the genuine proportion of their heritage will be found in the groundbreaking impacts they've had on the worldwide stage motivating ages to come. In a world that continually develops, KD's standards give a system to exploring the difficulties that lie ahead. As we close this part on the tradition of KD, obviously it isn't just about the past or present achievements yet the future prospects they have gotten rolling. Proceeding with commitment to initiative, development, and social advancement, KD's work will stay persevering through demonstration of the force of a solitary vision and the immovable effect of direction driven authority. Looking forward, this heritage is something beyond a memory, it's a living power. The standards KD supported will proceed to motivate and provoke the world to take a stab at a more comprehensive, creative, and versatile future. The effect of their authority will be found in each area, each local area, and each person who hopes against hope large and makes a move.

CONCLUSION

KD's excursion, chronicled all through these pages, is a festival of steadiness, versatility, and a resolute obligation to reason. The story isn't only one of individual victory however an impression of the widespread insights that guide the people who hope against hope past their conditions. From the beginning of vulnerability and challenge to snapshots of significant victory, KD's life embodies the ups and downs that characterize each uncommon account. At its center, this story is about the effect one individual can make when driven by both vision and respectability. KD's ascent is an update that initiative isn't about power or position however about the capacity to move, guide, and elevate others. The inheritance they have fabricated fills in as a guide for anybody endeavoring to leave the world a preferred spot over which they tracked it down. Their story, set apart by lowliness and persevering aspiration, resounds a long ways past their nearby effective reach, contacting lives and forming networks. The Accounts uncover the public achievements as well as the confidential fights that formed KD's personality. It is in these calmer, concealed minutes that the embodiment of genuine significance arises. This story exhibits that achievement isn't about an objective yet a ceaseless excursion of picking up, adjusting, and developing. As the story closes, it leaves us with a significant feeling of motivation and trust. KD's life advises us that our true capacity isn't restricted by our starting points or the difficulties we face. It is characterized by our readiness to push forward, to dream, and to lead with reason. This heritage, one based on values, vision, and unwavering assurance, will keep on rousing ages to come. KD's ascent isn't simply a story to be recalled, it is a source of inspiration for all who try to make a significant effect in their own daily routines and the existence of others.

Made in the USA
Columbia, SC
30 November 2024